REVOLUTION

Your Financial Revolution
THE POWER OF REST

GARY KEESEE

Your Financial Revolution:
The Power of Rest

ISBN: 978-1-945930-03-4

Published by Free Indeed Publishers.
Distributed by Faith Life Now.

Faith Life Now
P.O. Box 779
New Albany, OH 43054
1-(888)-391-LIFE

You can reach Faith Life Now Ministries on the Internet at www.faithlifenow.com.

I want to dedicate this book to my wife, Drenda, as it has been her encouragement, her passion for the things of God, and her love for her family and me that has inspired me all of these years. Together, we have proved that dreams really do come true!

Gary Keesee

TABLE OF CONTENTS

INTRODUCTION..9

CHAPTER 1: Rest - The Basics....................................... 13

CHAPTER 2: Legal Rights.. 27

CHAPTER 3: The Kingdom Is Your Answer.............................. 47

CHAPTER 4: I Found a Major Key of the Kingdom!................. 67

CHAPTER 5: Flying Is Better Than Walking.............................81

CHAPTER 6: There Is More to Life Than Paying the Bills!..........101

CHAPTER 7: This Is Impossible!....................................113

CHAPTER 8: The Double Portion....................................125

CHAPTER 9: More Than Enough!....................................139

CHAPTER 10: The Mystery of the Double Portion.................. 161

INTRODUCTION

The day we left the farmhouse was a bittersweet kind of day. We had lived in that old, tiny, run-down farmhouse for nearly nine years, and now I was carrying the last load of boxes out to our van. I was heading to our new home we had built ourselves, a 7,700 square foot, Georgian home that sat on 55 acres of beautiful Ohio farmland, with 20 acres of woods and marshes. It was a dream that would have been hard to imagine just a few years earlier.

Even though we were leaving the farmhouse, I loved that old house. Yes, even with its broken windowpanes, its dirt cellar, and the constant bee attacks we endured while we lived there. So many memories came to mind. Two of my five children were actually born there in the family room.

We had many good times there but also many times of financial stress and hopelessness. There were so many things we had to learn. Although hard to imagine now, when we moved into that old farmhouse nine years earlier, we could barely pay the $300 a month rent. Both of our cars were very old, with hundreds of thousands of miles on them, and yet they still had liens against them. At that time, it seemed we owed everyone money. We had ten maxed out and canceled credit cards; two finance company loans; of course, our two car payments;

IRS liens; the tens of thousands we owed our relatives; and the list goes on. We lived a life of financial survival, pawning most everything we owned sometimes just to buy groceries. The things we owned were very old and broken things we had purchased very old to begin with.

Our dire financial situation at the time held little hope for a bright future. Quite frankly, I did not see much hope things could change. I loved my family, I had a beautiful wife, but I was dragging them through financial hell!

I was on antidepressants, dealing with panic attacks, and fear consumed my daily life. Let's just say I wasn't the happiest person to be around. I was selling life insurance, living on commissions, and going nowhere fast, except further into a financial abyss. Slowly, we were getting further and further in debt until there were no more debt options left. It was at this point I crashed emotionally. Panic and fear overtook my mind. I was even afraid of leaving my house, which by the way is not good for commission sales.

My wife thought she was going to lose her husband, and the fear of raising the four children we had at the time alone haunted her. But she is a strong believer in the power of prayer and did not give up on me. Together, we prayed and then set out to discover the principles of God's Kingdom. As we began to seek God for answers and principles, hope began to rise in our hearts as we saw one miracle after another when we applied what God showed us.

A defining moment occurred one night as God showed me that I was to start my own company in the financial field helping people get out of debt and teaching them the principles He was showing me. At the time, starting a company showing people how to get out of debt seemed rather strange as we still had a lot of debt ourselves. We prayed about this, but the Lord told us that as we stepped out and began teaching His principles, we would find our freedom as well. Starting the company was a walk of faith since we had no clue how to do that, but we persevered at it. The company grew, and the money it brought in brought our family completely out of debt in two and half years. I will talk a bit more on our company in the next chapter, but for now, just know that our lives changed drastically! There is no way I can explain how we felt to be free, how it felt to walk into a car dealership and pay cash for a new car. How it felt to design, build, and pay for our new home. What we were enjoying was beyond anything we could have imagined.

Yes, the farmhouse held quite a few memories. As I went to grab the last box from the house, I passed my wife as she stood in the little dining room. She looked up at me with tears in her eyes. They were not sad tears; they were tears of joy and also tears of emotion, as she remembered all that God had taught us there. I fought back tears also as I took one last look through the rooms, remembering with mixed emotions everything that had taken place there. We were closing a chapter in our lives and going on to new territory. What was before us now? The journey had taken us from depression, with no hope, to a future full of hope. As I went

AS WE BEGAN TO SEEK GOD FOR ANSWERS AND PRINCIPLES, HOPE BEGAN TO RISE IN OUR HEARTS AS WE SAW ONE MIRACLE AFTER ANOTHER WHEN WE APPLIED WHAT GOD SHOWED US.

outside with the last box, I stopped and looked back at the house with a smile. "No, I will not miss you. I have a better place now."

It was thrilling to be moving to our new home for sure. But the best thing about our journey was there was finally rest! I could think about my future and not just about paying the bills. Over the years, living in His rest has been an absolute dream! Having our cars paid for is rest. Being debt free is rest. Having my dream home on 55 acres paid for is rest. Seeing the smile on my wife's face when she goes shopping and doesn't have to worry about money is rest. Beyond having all that we need, having enough money to be able to give hundreds of thousands of dollars to others and to support the Gospel is rest. But probably the greatest change in my life was not waking up every day to the pressure and fear that surrounded my life all those early years. Being able to dream again of good things instead of dreaming of just surviving one more week is rest.

WHAT DRENDA AND I DISCOVERED IS JUST AS MUCH AVAILABLE TO YOU AS IT WAS TO US.

Yes, the day I was packing the last boxes into the van to take the trip to our new home was bittersweet. But trust me, the sweetness of the rest that Drenda and I discovered so overpowered the bitter thoughts of leaving those memories behind that we felt like two little school-age kids again, laughing and dreaming together.

I know what you are thinking. I wish I had that. I wish I could have that experience and laugh, dream, and be able to focus on something other than just paying the bills. Although you may find it hard to believe at this point in the book, I assure you that what Drenda and I discovered is just as much available to you as it was to us. My prayer is as we share our story, you will be encouraged to apply God's laws and principles to your own life as well.

It really is not that hard; you simply need to discover the power of rest!

> *Come to me, all you who are weary and burdened, and I will give you rest. Take my yoke upon you and learn from me, for I am gentle and humble in heart, and you will find rest for your souls. For my yoke is easy and my burden is light.*
> — Matthew 11:28-30

CHAPTER 1
REST - THE BASICS

REST - to be placed or supported so as to stay in a specified position, an instance or period of relaxing or ceasing to engage in strenuous or stressful activity. (Google.)

Are you tired? Are you overwhelmed most days and never get caught up? Is your need for money driving your decisions as to where you work or how you work or how long you work? Does it seem that you will never get out of debt? Does it seem you are living the proverbial rat race? If this is you, you are not alone.

Have you ever seen a hamster wheel? I am sure you have, but in case you have not, it is a wheel that is put in a hamster cage. The hamster can get on that wheel and run and run and run until he is worn out. But there is only one problem with that wheel. No matter how fast or how long that hamster runs, when he is good and tired and gets off, he is in the exact same place he started from. Nothing has changed. He can wipe the sweat from his furry little face with a satisfied feeling. But nothing was accomplished to benefit his position in life; he is still locked up in a cage with no freedom. This pretty much sums up many people, if not the majority of people, and their financial lives. They work hard all week and fall exhausted into a brief diversion on the weekend, but when Monday morning comes around, they find themselves in the exact same location as they were the week before. All they have done is survived one more week.

This was a picture of my life for nine long years. I was putting in 15 to 18 hours a day, I was diligent, and I worked hard, but after I paid my tithe, my bills, and taxes, there was nothing left. Usually, I was short of what I needed and slowly began a habit of borrowing to survive. When the financial pressure would increase, I would run all the harder, but to no avail. When I stopped and judged my progress, I was still moving backwards.

This, of course, led to some severe emotional consequences. The discouragement and fear I battled every day slowly affected my mind and my physical body. Panic attacks, intense fear, and paralysis slowly began taking over my body. Doctors could not find out what was wrong with me. Fear so consumed my thoughts that I did not know if I would live or die. Living out of pawnshops and borrowing money from relatives went on for almost nine years! By that time, there was nothing else to pawn, and there was little of my self-image left. I was done. You could have scooped up my self-image with a dustpan, along with any joy that was left in life.

Creditors were lining up to file against me, and that is when it happened. With hopelessness embracing my every breath, the call came. The call came in like most other morning calls: "Mr. Keesee, as you know, you owe our client X amount of money. When do you think you can get this to us? Well, Mr. Keesee, you said that the last three times I called you. If you do not have the money to us in three days, my client will be filing a lawsuit for this debt against you. Do you understand, Mr. Keesee? Three days. Good-bye."

The call hit me like a ton of bricks. Not that I already did not know how dire our financial situation was. I had no money. Everything I owned was broken. My refrigerator was empty. My beautiful family was sleeping by the fireplace to keep warm as there was no money for heating oil. I had nowhere to turn. My friends and family were tired of paying my way. Confused, I slowly made my way up the stairs to my bedroom and laid across the bed. I sobbed and cried out to the Lord for help.

I think I was surprised how fast the Lord spoke to me. It was not an audible voice but a voice that suddenly came up out of my spirit and into my mind with force. The first thing the Lord said to me was that the mess I was in had nothing to do with Him. I suppose He said that because I was a little confused as to why He, from my perspective, had not helped us. We went to a great church, were generous when we could be, and paid our tithes most of the time. Instead, He said the reason I was in this mess was because I had never learned how His Kingdom operated. He told me that His Kingdom does not operate like the earth realm operates in regard to money, and I would have to learn His Kingdom system of handling finances if I wanted to be free.

I remember running downstairs and grabbing Drenda and telling her that the Lord had just spoken to me and that the answer was His Kingdom. Of course, we were a little confused, as we thought we understood what His Kingdom was. After all, as I said, we went to a great church, we both loved God, and knew we were on our way to heaven. But as we were about to find out, we really knew very little about His Kingdom and how it operated.

I was excited that God had spoken to me and that He had revealed the answer—His Kingdom. What that meant was yet to be grasped, but I was encouraged. The reality was that I had no clue what God meant by the word *kingdom*. I was to find out that in that one word was indeed the answer that Drenda and I had been longing and searching for.

Drenda and I joined hands that day and prayed. First, we repented to God for not taking the time to really learn his Word and how His Kingdom operated in regard to finances. Secondly, I repented to her, as the head of the family, for getting us into this mess. We both prayed and agreed that we were determined to learn how the Kingdom operated and to live a different life than the one we had been living for the last nine years.

The best way to describe what happened next is to look at a light switch. Walk into a room that is dark and simply flip the switch. Light! You can see. That is what it was like when God began to teach us His Kingdom. It was like someone turned on a light switch, and we could see things that we have never seen before. We began to understand that the Kingdom of God is a government with laws that do not change. We realized that we could learn those laws and tap into God's power and wisdom to create the wealth we needed.

We were so excited but yet still very much confused. There were some pretty amazing stories that took place as God began to teach us how His Kingdom operated. I am not going to cover many of those early stories here as they are covered in the first book in this series, *Your Financial Revolution: The Power of Allegiance*. You can get a copy at garykeesee.com or at Amazon.com. You also need to get my book, *Faith Hunt*, which takes you back to the very beginning as God began to teach me how to harvest provision through my deer hunting. But to make a long story short, let me give you one example here.

As I have told you, we were up to our eyeballs in debt with no way out. IRS liens, pawnshops, 10 maxed out and canceled credit cards, and 3 finance company loans at 28% interest. We owed our dentist, the dry cleaners, our parents, and our friends. You name it, we owed them. In the natural, there was no hope. My financial sales business was not going well, although I worked hard. But now after seeing the Kingdom do some pretty incredible things (again, read the stories in the two books mentioned above), we were encouraged that the Kingdom was our answer. We had no clue how, but we were confident that we were on the right path.

Then one night God gave me a dream and showed me in that dream that I was to leave my current company I had been with for the last nine years and start my own company—now get this—to help people get out of debt! I know; crazy, right? I mean, if I had known how to get out of debt, I would have done it years earlier. But that is exactly what He did. I was a little shocked actually. I had no idea how to start my own company or what was involved. But a company to help people get out of debt? Hey, I still needed someone to tell me how to do that!

As I began to pray about this, I had a life-changing experience with the Holy Spirit in regard to just how this could happen. It happened at one of my client calls for my insurance business. Oh, I forgot to tell you that I was in the financial services industry selling insurance and securities while all this happened. I know, it is kind of like the plumber with the leaky faucet taking care of everyone else's problem but neglecting his own. Although I was slowly failing in my financial services position, the experience I had gained in general knowledge in that field over the previous nine years was now very important to what God was about to show me.

As I was sitting down with my client and his wife at their kitchen table, we went through the usual presentation, which took a snapshot of where they were financially by asking various questions and filling out what we called a data sheet. This data was used primarily to determine just how much life insurance they should have. As we were going through their list of debts, they both became upset and the wife began to cry as they described how hopeless they both felt.

They were both working full-time jobs and were falling short every month.

Now, after living that way for nine years myself, and with God beginning to teach Drenda and me about the Kingdom, you can imagine how I felt for them. Like Drenda and I, they were Christians but with no knowledge of how the Kingdom operated. At the time, I really could not explain much about the Kingdom except some of the initial things God had already showed us, which I shared with them, and, of course, I shared some of the amazing stories we had seen happen in our own situation.

Obviously, I could tell that life insurance was not their major problem. I spent some time explaining what God was teaching me concerning the Kingdom, but I longed for something I could do to also offer real financial answers regarding their situation.

At the office that night, as I was wrapping up my day and sorting through my normal pile of files and messages that I needed to return, I suddenly had a thought. What if I looked past the life insurance issue and took a long look at their entire financial picture? Was there anything I could do? What if I began to look for money? What I mean by that is what if I could find cheaper ways to do things that they were already doing? My goal would be simple, find cheaper ways to do things they were already doing and then apply any money I found to their cash flow and debt. It sounded like a simple proposition, but I really did not know much about any other financial field outside of life insurance. And I need to tell you that this was before the days of the Internet. The research that I would need to do would be done the old-fashioned way—by phone and the yellow pages.

I worked on this the entire week as I was scheduled to meet this client again the following week. I was surprised with just how much money I could free up a month as I took the time to really dig into each financial area. By the time I was finished, the amount added up to hundreds of dollars a month. With my financial calculator, I added up all of their debts and then applied the freed up money to their normal monthly payments. When I hit the compute button, I just stared at the answer on the screen—6.2 years. The answer of 6.2 years was the total time it would take for my client to pay off all of his debt, including his home mortgage, without changing his income. Yes, you read that right, without changing his monthly income. I was shocked and convinced I had made a mistake, so I did the math over and over again until I was convinced that I had the right answer. Could this be? Why didn't everyone know this?

I quickly grabbed a few other clients' files I had on hand and did a quick scan with them and found the same results. Every one of them could be out of debt in 5 to 7 years, including their mortgage, without changing their monthly income. It was now getting late at the office as I finished up my calculations, but as I headed home I was excited. If what I found was true, and all my calculations indicated that it was, then this was big, really big.

I was curious how my client might respond to this kind of information. For my upcoming appointment, I decided to type up the numbers into a simple one-page presentation. My objective was to simply give them hope. There was nothing in it for me, as I knew that a possible life insurance sale was unlikely. But I also knew they would want to hear what I had found out. The following week I again reviewed my calculations and was sure I was right.

As I rang the doorbell, I felt a nervous anticipation to our meeting. As I sat down at their kitchen table, I told them what I had done all week with their numbers. I slowly walked them through the numbers I had typed up, explaining how I had come up with the freed up cash, along with any company name and number that would be needed to implement what I had shown them. I could tell that they were getting excited as the freed up cash kept growing. But when I came to the conclusion of being completely out of debt in 6.2 years, including their home, on their current income, they both began to cry, this time with joy. They sat there with tears streaming down their faces and just kept saying how shocked they were at the results. They jumped up and gave me a hug, and we had a great time of celebration that night.

Let's be honest: Is the IRS going to tell you how to pay less taxes? Is the banker going to tell you how to avoid paying interest? No, the whole system is designed to take your money, not to protect it. I knew that what I had discovered needed to be taught to every family in America! That night had a dramatic impact on me, and I wanted to do the same thing for every client I met.

So, armed with that information and with the confirmation of the dream God gave me, Drenda and I left the life insurance company that I worked with and launched our own company, doing just what I had done for that client. In those early years, we called our company, "Faith-Full Family Finances." The name clearly said what we were all about—if you understood the Kingdom and faith, your finances would be full. I agree it was not a very good name for a company—try saying it ten times in a row—but it worked. We later changed the name to Forward Financial Group, which it is today and is still going strong.

To be honest, personally, our finances were not yet full. We still had all those debts to pay, but we knew we had found our track to run on. As we launched out with our new company, we were excited and a bit nervous at the same time. We had a lot to learn about setting up and running a company, but the biggest hurdle we faced was how to make any money doing it. Our challenge was we felt we could not, and we did not want to charge people money to help them get out of debt. This was a big hurdle which we spent quite a bit of time praying about and looking at options. Without going into detail, the Lord showed us an amazing strategy to set up the company and posture it to make money without charging the client a fee.

Next, we had to find a way to speed up the lengthy hand calculations I was doing with my clients' data. I knew that I would have to custom write a computer program to do what we were doing, but I knew nothing about computers or how to find someone who had the ability to do that. Again, God did some amazing work. I received a call from a person a long way from our home who had heard of us. He wanted to see what we did, as a client. He loved what we did, and as we were talking, I found out that he was a computer programmer and had his own company on the side part-time. I talked to him about our need, and he very enthusiastically said he wanted to help us with what we were doing. I told him that we were just starting our company and we did not have the funds yet to pay for the work he had offered, even though he had offered his work at a huge discount. He still wanted to do the work and said I could pay him whenever the money came in. So that is what we did.

People loved our business. After all, why not? It was free, and people liked finding money and getting out of debt. The business took off in a big way, and we were able to become debt free in two and a half years. Soon we had over 300 representatives sharing our plan all over the country. Besides being able to pay cash for our cars, we went on to build and pay for our dream home. Our company grew and has enabled us to give hundreds of thousands of dollars away to support the Gospel and people over the years.

The "debt plan," as we call it, is still produced today for free, 30 years later. The company grew in its mission as the years went by.

We went on to focus on retirement investing after the 2001 financial crash and then, of course, the 2008 crash where millions of people lost 50% to 80% of their retirement savings. We researched safe investing options and launched that aspect of our business in 2001. I am proud to say that of the over one hundred million dollars we currently manage for our clients, not one of them lost one penny in their investments over the previous 16 years of financial chaos in our country and the world. And like our plan, there is no fee, no administration fee or broker fee involved initially or yearly for our investment clients. If you are tired of gambling with your retirement money, you can reach Forward Financial Group at 1-(800)-815-0818 or Forwardfinancialgroup.com for more information.

Amazing isn't it? One simple idea from the Holy Spirit changed our lives forever! Yes, we had to walk it out, but God showed us where to walk. "How did it feel, Gary, to be out of debt?" Peace! Rest! Think about it. We went from being in severe financial dysfunction to being completely out of debt, paying cash for our cars, our home, and everything else we needed. For nine long years, I was under extreme pressure every minute of every day. I had no rest. It did not matter what day of the week it was, or if it was a holiday. I was not at peace. My financial issues followed me everywhere I went. I endured constant embarrassment and humiliation due to our financial condition. Fear was my constant companion, panic attacks and antidepressants a way of life at the height of my despair.

With all the financial changes, and of course having the things we needed in life in place, you may be tempted to think that in and of itself our personal finances were the victory. Yes, finally having the things we needed was a huge victory, but the real excitement was to see the Kingdom of God operate. As Drenda and I saw the Kingdom function again and again, we would often say, "Did you see that?"

Just like a light switch being turned on, everything is clear in the light; you can see. Being able to see after you have been blind and living with no answers is a wonderful experience. Finding our true treasure, the Kingdom of God, was simply amazing. To try to tell you how it felt is simple— for the first time in my life, there was rest!

ONE SIMPLE IDEA FROM THE HOLY SPIRIT CHANGED OUR LIVES FOREVER! YES, WE HAD TO WALK IT OUT, BUT GOD SHOWED US WHERE TO WALK.

The drama stopped! In the past, if our tire blew out, it became a major emotional crisis. "Where will we get the money? Is there any room left on the cards?" But today, if for some reason the car blew up, I would just ask my wife, "What color do you want this time?" No drama, no panic, no debt, just rest. We can stay on assignment and on our purpose. No longer living a life of survival, we can be about LIFE!

> *Therefore I tell you, do not worry about your life, what you will eat or drink; or about your body, what you will wear. Is not life more important than food, and the body more important than clothes? Look at the birds of the air; they do not sow or reap or store away in barns, and yet your heavenly Father feeds them. Are you not much more valuable than they?*
>
> — Matthew 6:25-26

Over these last 36 years, I have sat down with thousands of people across their kitchen tables and discussed their finances on a very personal level. I have talked to crowds of thousands all over the world, and the one thing I find everywhere I look is that everyone is looking for rest!!!!! Everyone looks forward to the weekend, to vacation, or to retirement—to stop and rest.

Several recent studies I read found that about 70% of Americans do not like their jobs, and of those 70%, 20% are not engaged and assumed to hate their jobs. Why do they show up to something that they hate? What kind of stress are they living under to put up with so much emotional pain on a daily basis? To put it bluntly, they are slaves. (We all were. We have grown up in a world where the only way to thrive is to have enough money to have options. But for most people, this just is not the case.) Their dreams of thriving slowly fade away to a life of survival as they find themselves in dead-end jobs in their 30s, 40s, and even 50s.

LIVING A LIFE OF FINANCIAL STRESS... WAS NOT GOD'S PLAN IN THE BEGINNING, AND IT IS NOT GOD'S PLAN FOR YOU TODAY EITHER.

A recent stat states that 69% of the American population does not even have one thousand dollars in savings[1]. The stress and emotional trauma that most people live under warps their sense of identity and self-worth. Dreams are shelved for urgent needs and a dull disillusionment takes over. The joy is gone.

One day, I remember talking to a pastor about finances. He told me that he loved the ministry and loved people, but every day he woke up with excitement until he remembered his financial situation. He told me it was like a big black cloud that cuts off the sunlight, as discouraging thoughts formed in his mind and held him hostage to a survival mind-set, financial hopelessness, and visionless slavery.

---

[1] Niall McCarthy, "Survey: 69% of Americans Have Less Than $1,000 in Savings," *Forbes*, September 23, 2016, https://www.forbes.com/sites/niallmccarthy/2016/09/23/survey-69-of-americans-have-less-than-1000-in-savings-infographic/#30d27351ae67.

Life has been replaced by watching others win. Hollywood has made billions showing the masses other people winning on the big screen. People who cannot see themselves winning personally find a few minutes of escape from their drudgery and live their dreams out by watching perfect people live perfect lives on the big screen.

Sports currently draw billions of dollars a year from spectators around the world. In 2017, the NFL brought in over 7.8 billion; the Super Bowl, an estimated 15.5 billion; and that is just one game![2] [3] People love cheering their favorite team on to victory.

But what we need to understand is that we all were destined and created to win—to be in the struggle, to be in the game, and ultimately to win. Financial hopelessness is the norm, not the exception, for most people—so the only escape is living the life we all dream of through the lives of others. What is the lure of winning the lottery? Why was the TV show *Who Wants To Be A Millionaire* so popular?" Why are get rich schemes still a temptation today? The answer? REST! Everyone is tired of running, everyone is tired of waking up with the weight of finding provision stealing their dreams. But living a life of financial stress is not something new; in fact, it has been around for about as long as man has been on the earth. However, it was not God's plan in the beginning, and it is not God's plan for you today either.

[2] Michael David Smith, "Packers' Books Show NFL teams Split $7.8 Billion in National Revenue," NBC Sports, http://profootballtalk.nbcsports.com/2017/07/12/packers-books-show-nfl-teams-split-7-8-billion-in-national-revenue/.

[3] Joe D'Allegro, "Super Bowl Billions: The Big Business Behind the Biggest Game of the Year," CNBC, January 22, 2017, updated February 2, 2017, https://www.cnbc.com/2017/01/20/super-bowl-billions-the-big-business-behind-the-big-game.html.

CHAPTER 2
LEGAL RIGHTS

Hopeless—that is how I would describe our lives before we understood how to rest. Nine years is a long time to live in financial chaos and stress. I can remember many times looking out over the 85-acre farm we rented for $300 a month, barely making that payment, which was extremely cheap, and wondering if I would ever be able to own land like this.

The owner was going to build a golf course on the property and just wanted someone to live there, to just watch over the property until they began the project, which they projected would be about three to five years away. The old farmhouse came "as is," and they would not pay for any repairs during that time. We took it, and after some serious painting and cleaning, the old house had its unique charm. Our plan was to stay there for three years then move on, but in our eighth year there, we were still no closer to owning anything.

After God spoke to me about the Kingdom, and we began to study and apply the principles and laws of the Kingdom, things began to change. In the beginning as our finances began to improve, we were so thrilled with the smallest victories. I can remember buying a dishwasher for the old farmhouse and Drenda and I were so happy, especially her! Although at times I did help out with washing the dishes, I also was busy with business. Having four children at home at the time, she always was washing dishes. When we bought the dishwasher, I can remember saying something like, "Can you believe that we just paid cash for a new dishwasher?" I know, you are thinking, "Wow, what is so big about buying a dishwasher?" Well, to put that into perspective, you would have to look at the other appliances in our farmhouse kitchen. Both our stove and refrigerator were avocado green and were 25 years old. So in comparison, buying a new dishwasher was a huge victory for us.

In the last chapter, I shared how God gave me a dream and a plan to launch a business that would become the answer to our financial chaos. You might be thinking, "I wish God would tell me something like that." The good news is that He desires to do so, but there are some things that you must know regarding how the Kingdom operates before you will able to tap into that kind of help. The direction I received that day in the dream only occurred because of what God was teaching us about His Kingdom and was a direct result of applying what He had shown us. Although I covered the Kingdom in great detail in my last book, I do need to review it here again to give us a platform from which to work.

People ask me what I mean by God's Kingdom. I had no knowledge of God's Kingdom even though I was a Christian. I knew I was going to heaven when I died, but I had no understanding of the Kingdom of God and how it actually functioned. To understand this concept, you need to understand what the word *kingdom* means. In a literal sense, it means the king's dominion. A king's kingdom operates by the word of the king. His words become the law that govern His domain and the lives of his citizens. Another concept involving a kingdom is that a mob of a million people does not make a kingdom. Kingdom infers a government with laws that enforce the king's laws to every legal citizen of that kingdom. This concept that God has a Kingdom with established laws that are available to every legal citizen of his Kingdom seems to be void in most of Christianity. Most Christians believe that God decides what prayers He answers or to whom He shows favoritism. They believe that if they fast for a very long time or do more spiritual work for God, then they will have favor with Him. My friend, you already have favor with Him.

> *Consequently, you are no longer foreigners and aliens, but fellow citizens with God's people and members of God's household.*
>
> — Ephesians 2:19

You are not only a citizen of his Kingdom, but also you are a member of His very own household, a son or daughter of the King. Galatians 4 makes very clear what this means to you and me.

> *What I am saying is that as long as an heir is a child, he is no different from a slave, although he owns the whole estate. He is subject to guardians and trustees until the time set by his father. So also, when we were children, we were in slavery under the basic principles of the world. But when the time had fully come, God sent his Son, born of a woman, born under law, to redeem those under law, that we might receive the full rights of sons. Because you are sons, God sent the Spirit of his Son into our hearts, the Spirit who calls out, "Abba, Father." So you are no longer a slave, but a son; and since you are a son, God has made you also an heir.*
>
> — Galatians 4:1-7

You are an heir of the entire estate as a son or daughter, and you have legal rights as a citizen of His Kingdom! Let that sink in for a minute—you already have the whole thing. There is nothing that you need that you do not already have. So stop the begging and the crying. You cannot beg for something that you already have. God does not make a case by case decision regarding who He will or won't help. Anyone who is a son or daughter of God already has His help.

FEELINGS ARE NICE, AND I LOVE TO FEEL GOD'S PRESENCE, BUT WHEN IT COMES TO LEGAL MATTERS, I DO NOT NEED TO FEEL SAVED TO BE SAVED. IT IS A LEGAL ISSUE.

Let me compare this to being a citizen of the United States. If you are a citizen, then you already have the backing of the United States government to enforce what the law says. That benefit was included with your citizenship. So, you can't fast and pray long enough to earn His help; He has given it to you freely through what Jesus did. So enjoy it. You own it!

> And God raised us up with Christ and seated us with him in the heavenly realms in Christ Jesus, in order that in the coming ages he might show the incomparable riches of his grace, expressed in his kindness to us in Christ Jesus.
>
> — Ephesians 2:6-7

That phrase, "*seated us with him in the heavenly realms*" is speaking of your legal position in God's Kingdom. Jesus is seated at the right hand of the Father, and so are you since you are the body of Christ. Thus you are a coheir with Jesus of all that God has. I know it is incredible to think of that, but it is true. You have it all; you are family, and it is the family business! But because the devil has tried to hide all that you are and all that you have, most people, even Christians, live as those still bound by the earth curse system of survival!

The key that changed my life was when I realized it was and is a government with laws and I, being a citizen, have legal rights and benefits in the Kingdom. Feelings are nice, and I love to feel God's presence, but when it comes to legal matters, I do not need to feel saved to be saved. It is a legal issue. I do not have to feel like I am a citizen of the United States to be one. I already know it is a legal matter that is satisfied by the fact that I was born here. When you're in right standing before God and your life is based on law instead of how you feel, things change!

> *This is the confidence we have in approaching God: that if we ask anything according to his will, he hears us. And if we know that he hears us—whatever we ask—we know that we have what we asked of him.*
>
> — 1 John 5:14-15

Think of this Scripture for a minute; it is one of my favorites. If I ask anything according to His will, I know He hears it! This is not referring to the audio sound waves you hear with your ears. This is a legal statement. Think of a judge and his courtroom. If a judge decides to hear a case, it means he has agreed to settle a matter based on what the laws says. In our case, since we have asked according to the laws of the King, we already know He will enforce His own law. Thus, we are confident in the outcome; there will be no guessing.

For instance, the United States is not a kingdom for it does not have a king, but it operates by laws that are equal for and available to every legal citizen. In a similar way, God's Kingdom is also governed by laws, which are available to every citizen without partiality. The stories we read in the Bible are not there just to amuse us but to illustrate those laws for us so that we can learn them and use them. Jesus used the phrase, "the Kingdom of God is like" many times as He was explaining to people how the Kingdom functioned. Jesus was referring to the laws of the Kingdom when He told the parables, giving a visual picture of how the laws worked or identifying why something happened. Again, for some reason, people have no concept of God's Kingdom having laws that govern its operation. Many think that God can do anything He wants to do when He wants to because He is God. I will agree that God has the power to do anything He wants to do; however, He is limited by His own laws. I know this may sound strange to you, but to make my point, let's take a quick look at Mark 6.

Jesus said to them, "Only in his hometown, among his relatives and in his own house is a prophet without honor." He could not do any miracles there, except lay his hands on a few sick people and heal them. And He was amazed at their lack of faith.
— Mark 6:4-6

As you read this Scripture, you should have had a couple of things jumping off the page at you that give you some insight into the function of the Kingdom.

He <u>could not</u> do any miracles....

First of all, many Christians have not even seen this Scripture and would argue with you up front that if you said there were situations in the Bible where Jesus could not heal, you would be wrong. But as you can see, He could not. Once you understand that the Kingdom operates by laws, then you begin to look deeper at this story. The standard understanding for most Christians would be that Jesus chose not to heal them. That would make logical sense if you had no understanding of the legality of the Kingdom. Knowing that Jesus had the power to heal yet did not, without an understanding of legal jurisdiction, you would naturally conclude that He chose not to heal. What else could it be?

You might have heard someone say, "God allowed this to happen," or "God knows best," or "God has it all in His control," or something along those lines when someone is referencing a problem or hardship either they or a friend are going through. For the general Christian, this is where they stop. Not knowing the laws of the Kingdom and what actually hindered Jesus, the only conclusion they can draw is that it must not have been God's will to heal them. My friend, the Bible does not say He chose not to heal. It says He could not heal them because of their lack of faith. Once you realize that the hindrance to healing in this story was not God's lack of desire to do so, but rather, that there were spiritual laws of jurisdiction that stopped the power of God.

In other stories, you now will realize that there were legal reasons why the power of God had the jurisdiction to bring His will and desire into a situation or not, just as in this one. Therefore, it is extremely urgent that you find out how these laws of the Kingdom work. Someday when you may need a touch from heaven, you do not want heaven's power to be short-circuited, but rather, to have the freedom to produce the will of God in your life. And that is exactly why I wrote this book.

To really begin your journey, I would recommend that you start with a clean slate in your mind and realize that you need to throw out the old religious answers you have heard all your life regarding why

God does or does not do something. I hope you now know that you need to reject the common explanation that is usually given when referring to why little Johnny died at a young age: "God knows best, He's in control," etc. No, you need to KNOW why Jesus could not heal and the laws that govern the flow of God's power in the earth realm. You need to know the answer to the question, "Why couldn't Jesus heal?" For most people, the fact that I even say there is an answer to that question causes them to be offended. But I am only telling you what the Bible says, and let me reiterate that you absolutely MUST know the answer to that question.

HIS PROMISES GIVE US A PROMISE OF HEALING, RESTORATION, FINANCIAL INCREASE, AND SO MUCH MORE—NOT OF JUST HAVING THE ABILITY TO SUFFER THROUGH HARDSHIP OR DISASTER.

The simple and short answer explaining why Jesus could not heal in that story is that heaven did not have the legal jurisdiction to do so. That jurisdiction is granted by faith by a man or woman in the earth realm being fully persuaded of what heaven says. Although we both would agree that Jesus had the power and the desire to heal the people, He could not. Jesus, Himself said that the failure to heal was not a weakness on His end but was because the people did not have faith. Write that down! There is a major key here! Faith!

In my previous book, I spent a great deal of time explaining what faith is, how it works, why we need faith, why God requires faith, how we get faith, and how we know if we are in faith. To say that your understanding of this most basic law of the Kingdom is important would be an understatement. It is life and death!

I recently received a newsletter from a well-known Christian ministry. Its contents were typical of what most Christians believe, unfortunately. Let me share some of it here.

It starts off with a great word from **Deuteronomy 31:6:**

> *Be strong and courageous. Do not be afraid or terrified because of them, for the Lord your God goes with you. He will never leave you nor forsake you.*

Then it goes on to say…

"Why doesn't God stop terrorism and suffering? Why does He allow people to die? Questions abound, and the truth of the matter is we just do not know all the answers. We don't know why God allows certain things to happen. What we do know is God's love is perfect. His ways are above our ways. We have to trust in His promises that tell us not that He will not give us more than we can handle, but that whatever He gives us, He will be with us each step of the way."

WRONG, WRONG, WRONG! In fact, the Bible tells us the exact opposite.

> *No temptation has overtaken you except such as is common to man; but God is faithful, who will not allow you to be tempted beyond what you are able, but with the temptation will also make the way of escape, that you may be able to bear it.*
>
> — 1 Corinthians 10:13 (NKJV)

His promises give us a promise of healing, restoration, financial increase, and so much more—not of just having the ability to suffer through hardship or disaster. Perfect love offers solutions. I could go on, but this, unfortunately, is what the majority of people believe about God. How someone could even think that God, whose love is perfect, would give a person cancer or refuse to heal them when He has the power to do so is beyond me. When asked about this, again, their usual response is that His ways are not our ways. Are you kidding? We do not have perfect love and we would not do that to our child! On the contrary, He makes His ways very plain in His Word.

The newsletter implied that whatever He gives us, He will be there each step of the way as we suffer through it. Is God going to give us something that is bad? No. When the Bible tells us that He is with us and will never leave us, it means that God is right there with us to back up His promises! My friend, this doctrine that God is our enemy is not from God. It does not represent the God I serve, and I hope you will not put up with it. If your church teaches this kind of garbage, you should leave immediately!

God is love and the Word says love never fails. What does fail, however, is God's jurisdiction, His ability to intervene in the earth realm, which is produced by our faith. Again, this is a legal issue, not a goose bump issue, a feeling issue, or anything else. It is simply a legal issue that you must know. Since man has jurisdiction in the earth realm, God cannot just do what He wants, as I have shared. Your agreement with heaven, your faith, is needed to give heaven jurisdiction to bring the power of God into that situation and produce righteousness. Friend, you **must** know what faith is and why it is needed to receive from God.

In case you have not read my previous book (*Your Financial Revolution: The Power of Allegiance*), let me review just briefly what faith is. Although you could assume that almost every Christian using the word *faith* would know what it is, you would be wrong. We need to have a little history lesson to be able to understand a vital Kingdom concept regarding legal jurisdiction.

Let's take a look **Romans 4:18-21:**

> *Against all hope, Abraham in hope believed and so became the father of many nations, just as it had been said to him, "So shall your offspring be." Without weakening in his faith, he faced the fact that his body was as good as dead—since he was about a hundred years old—and that Sarah's womb was also dead. Yet he did not waver through unbelief regarding the promise of God, but was strengthened in his faith and gave glory to God, being fully persuaded that God had power to do what he had promised.*

Abraham is known as the father of our faith. He was fully persuaded that God had power to do what He had promised. Being fully persuaded, in agreement with God, is called faith. Without that agreement, God cannot move in the earth realm. So you may ask, "Why would God need anyone to do anything which would allow Him to do something or hinder Him from doing whatever He so chooses? He is God." To answer that question, we need to take a quick look back at the beginning, during Adam's time.

> *You made him a little lower than the angels; you crowned him with glory and honor and put everything under his feet. In putting everything under him, God left <u>nothing that is not subject to him</u>. Yet at present we do not see everything subject to him.*
>
> — Hebrews 2:7-8

This Scripture is referring to Adam and Eve at creation. Please note that there was nothing on the earth that was not under their legal jurisdiction. Adam was placed on the earth to rule the earth with delegated authority on behalf of the Kingdom of God. He ruled the entire earth.

> *Then God said, "Let us make man in our image, in our likeness, and <u>let them rule</u> over the fish of the sea and the birds of the air, over the livestock, over all the earth, and over all the creatures that move along the ground."*
>
> — Genesis 1:26

So again, we see that Adam ruled the earth with delegated authority and was crowned with glory (the anointing or power) and honor (the position of authority). There was nothing that was not under his domain. In fact, if you read the creation account, Adam actually named the animals, as he was over the whole planet. As we all know, Adam lost his place of authority over Satan, who deceived Eve and tempted Adam to commit treason against the government of God, which he did. Paul records in 2 Corinthians 4:4 that Satan, through Adam's treason, became the god of this world. He did not say he was a god, but rather, the god of this world, meaning he had the legal spiritual authority here. Although man still lived on the earth, spiritually, he was dead to God. Man's spirit, which was created to walk in union with God's Spirit, was now separated from Him. Man began to walk according to his own senses, his mind, will, and emotions.

> *The devil led him up to a high place and showed him in an instant all the kingdoms of the world. And he said to him, "I will give you all their authority and splendor; it has been given to me, and I can give it to anyone I want to. If you worship me, it will all be yours."*
>
> — Luke 4:5-7

You will notice that Satan says that the position that he holds over the earth realm was "**given**" to him. Of course, we know that the one that gave it to him was the one that legally possessed it in the beginning, which was Adam. This is important. If, in fact, Satan had tried to break into the earth realm illegally, he would have been instantly and forcibly thrown out. If you can think of a police officer calling for backup, you will have a good idea of why I am saying Satan would have been forced out. The badge the officer wears implies that the entire force and power of the United States government is there to back up his words.

The crown that Adam wore (the position he held), ruling on behalf of the government of God, brought all the power of God to back him up. Because of Adam's position on the earth, Satan had no jurisdiction in the earth realm whatsoever. He was ruled over by Adam and Eve. Satan's only legal means to gain jurisdiction in the earth realm would require Adam to take off his crown, which Satan had no authority to force him to do. Satan knew the only person that could take that crown off of Adam's head was Adam himself. That is why Satan had to resort to his plan of deception. What was that deception? Satan implied that God was not trustworthy and did not have their best interest at heart. He convinced Eve that there was benefit in disobeying God and that God's laws were holding her and Adam back from something beneficial.

Satan had to get Adam and Eve to believe or align themselves with him instead of God.

In simple terms, this is faith. Faith can be defined as being "fully persuaded" of what God says. Adam and Eve abandoned God's Word as reliable and came into agreement with what Satan said instead. They then acted on their belief, which nullified their right standing in the Kingdom of God and gave Satan a legal foothold over the affairs of men. The result? Adam, who had the authority over the earth realm, spiritually kicked God out when he aligned himself with Satan! Adam abandoned his crown, his place of authority, to follow Satan. In so doing, he basically kicked God out of his life. Many people would say, "No, it could not happen; Adam couldn't kick God out of the earth realm!" But as far as the affairs of men were concerned, he certainly did. Let me prove that to you. Let's look at **Genesis 3:17-19** again. After Adam had sinned, God went to him and said,

> *Cursed is the ground because of you, through painful toil you will eat of it all the days of your life. It will produce thorns and thistles for you, and you will eat the plants of the field. By the sweat of your brow you will eat your food until you return to the ground.*

Notice it says, "*Cursed is the ground [earth] because of you.*"

To be cursed simply means the absence of God's presence and blessing. It was Adam, who had the authority over the earth, who cut off God's legal jurisdiction in the earth realm. Basically, God is saying, "Hey, Adam, because of you, my hands have been tied. I cannot help you." He then tells Adam that his survival will now be up to him, with hard labor and painful toil. I call this the "earth curse system" of survival. This is where we all grew up—in the kingdom of survival and fear. We learned to worry, and fear has dominated our thoughts since we were born. I want to come back to this Scripture in just a bit to discuss the earth curse system further, but for now, I want to make sure you understand how Satan gained access into the earth realm. Again, he had to find a man or woman in the earth realm who had the God-given legal jurisdiction in the earth realm to open the door for him. Adam had that key, and Satan managed to deceive Adam into opening that door. Now, let's look at Hebrews 2:7-8 again.

> *You made him a little lower than the angels; you crowned him with glory and honor and put everything under his feet. In putting everything under him, God left nothing that <u>is</u> not subject to him. Yet at present we do not see everything subject to him.*
>
> — Hebrews 2:7-8

Notice that this Scripture states that God left nothing that IS not subject to him. Although this Scripture is referring to an event from long ago, it uses the word *is* in the present tense to describe man's current status on the earth. Although man lost his spiritual authority in the earth realm through Adam's sin, man did not lose his legal occupation of the earth itself, thus the usage of the word *is*. Because of this legal standing that man has on the earth, and because of Satan's legal spiritual stronghold on men, God cannot just come bursting into the earth realm and violate His own Word or Satan would claim foul.

God has to find a man or a woman in the earth realm who will come into agreement with Him, which opens the spiritual door for the Kingdom of God to have legal jurisdiction here. Just like Satan had to work through the gatekeeper, Adam, God now has to work through men and woman, the gatekeepers of the earth, to give the Kingdom jurisdiction here. Having your heart and mind fully persuaded of what heaven says is called faith. Faith must be present for the Kingdom of God to have jurisdiction here. I'm not going to take the time here to explain how to get faith or how to know if you are in faith. All of this is covered in my first book in this series. For the purpose of this discussion, I just want to make sure you know what faith is and why it is required for heaven to move here in the earth realm.

Now, I hope you have a better understanding of why Jesus "could not" do many miracles in His hometown—the people there did not have faith. Thus, heaven had no legal jurisdiction. Let me end this discussion with a great Scripture that will illustrate what I am saying.

Everyone has heard of Romans 10:10:

> *For it is with your heart that you believe and are justified, and it is with your mouth that you confess faith and are saved.*

This Scripture is part of what Christians call the Roman road, a part of four Scriptures that show us how to be saved. But have you really stopped and thought about the process Romans 10:10 is showing you? It is with your heart that you believe or come into agreement with heaven. Your heart being in agreement with heaven makes it legal for heaven to invade earth. This Scripture says when you believe heaven, you are justified. Justice is the administration of law. So believing in your heart gives you a legal right before heaven and earth to have what heaven says because it gives heaven legality in the earth realm. But notice nothing happens yet. There is a second part to this Scripture: "...*and it is with your mouth that you confess your faith and are saved.*" You see, although your heart can be in agreement with heaven, which makes it legal for heaven to invade earth, nothing happens until you, a man or a woman in the earth realm who has the jurisdiction over the earth realm, releases that into the earth realm. Why? Because you have jurisdiction here; heaven does not without you!

I tell you the truth, whatever you bind on earth will be bound in heaven, and whatever you loose on earth will be loosed in heaven.

— Matthew 18:18

Basically, this is saying what I have just talked about. Whatever you bind on earth, heaven will back up, and whatever you loose on earth, heaven will back up. Heaven cannot do it without you. Heaven is waiting on you and cannot move unless a man or woman who is in faith or agreement with heaven releases that authority into the earth realm.

Understanding how to release heaven's authority and power into the earth realm makes all the difference. It did in my life and it did in the following email I received.

"Hi! My husband and I want to share our amazing 'faith hunt' story with you! In 2011, we were living in our 'dream home,' but we were living paycheck to paycheck and at times using our credit cards to pay for groceries and [to] heat our house. We were surviving but not thriving. I was the worship leader in our church, but our faith was not connected to our finances. I saw your program *Fixing the Money Thing* on Daystar, which caught my attention, and [I] ordered the book, *Fixing the Money Thing*, along with the *Financial Revolution* CDs. We listened all the time to these CDs and read the book to each other.

"We had no idea we were not in faith! We knew that in order to keep this dream house, we needed some answers on how money operated in the Kingdom. We sowed a seed of $200 into Faith Life Ministries (which might as well [have] been $2,000. That was a lot of money to us then!) and came into agreement with God to show us a niche in the marketplace that I could do at home.

"God gave us a business idea of raising Goldendoodle puppies from our home. We purchased 2 Goldendoodle puppies, Bella and Gracie, raised them to breed Goldendoodle puppies, and we partnered with God. We knew we could not make puppies!! We bred our 2 doodles, and in 2014, we had 13 puppies to sell at a market price of $1200 each. This year, 2015, we have had 63 puppies, ALL healthy. From selling our puppies, we have become free from all our debt except our home. We also now had a fully funded emergency fund as well.

"To our surprise, my mom asked us if we would like her two Goldendoodles to breed because she was retiring! God blessed us with another 2 doodles free! And in July, my husband got promoted to high school superintendent at our local high school!! In one year, our income doubled to the high 6 figures!! FAITH HUNT WORKS!! We tapped into the laws of the Kingdom of God. Now, we sow into all kinds of Kingdom work and attend your church online every Sunday morning before we lead worship in our local church! Thank you for teaching us how the Kingdom operates!"

—Karla

This same couple sent me a follow up email this week.

"Happy Easter! He is risen! We wanted to share an update for our online Pastor Gary! Please let him know we celebrated the birth of Jesus in Jerusalem this year (paid for in cash). We were also blessed to have our teenage son Carter baptized in the Jordan River, and worshipped with Hillsong Australia at the Sea of Galilee in the evening! Wow!!! So thankful we fixed the money thing!

We have had 121 puppies now. We had to raise the price of a puppy to $2,300 because our waiting list was too long! Praise God."

—Karla

This is a perfect example of what the Kingdom will do in your life. I gave Karla a call this week after receiving this email, and she was SO excited!!! She said they will have their home paid off this year. If you look at the first email she sent, she said at that time the following (quoted from the above email):

"We were living paycheck to paycheck and at times using our credit cards to pay for groceries and [to] heat our house. We were surviving but not thriving."

Now, just a couple of years later, they will have it paid for? The Kingdom!

CHAPTER 3
THE KINGDOM IS YOUR ANSWER

Now that you have a basic understanding of how the Kingdom operates by laws and principles that never change, I want to start focusing on the laws that actually have an impact on your finances and, ultimately, your rest.

But before we go there, I want to define why I named this book *The Power of Rest* and what I mean by the word *rest* in the context of finances and the Kingdom. Surprisingly, I did not coin this concept as far as rest relates to finances, God did.

> *Thus the heavens and the earth were <u>completed</u> in all their vast array. By the seventh day God had <u>finished</u> the work he had been doing; so on the seventh day he <u>rested</u> from all his work. And God blessed the seventh day and made it holy, because on it he rested from all the work of creating that he had done.*
> — Genesis 2:1-3

First, let me make this clear: God did not rest on the seventh day because He was tired. God does not get tired. He rested because, as the text says, everything was complete and He was finished. He created man at the end of the sixth day of creation to live in the seventh day. The seventh day had no thought of fear, survival thinking, sickness, and no painful labor or sweat to obtain provision. Instead, Adam's thoughts would only be on God, his wife, his assignment, and purpose. Everything he needed to support his assignment and life were prepared and available; God's plan was complete. People today dream of having what Adam had, an existence free from care, having the ability to focus on their passions and relationships with no concern about provision. Unfortunately, when Adam rebelled, he lost God's provision, and man has been forced to run (painful toil and sweat) after the things of life ever since.

> For the pagans _run_ after all these things, and your heavenly Father knows that you need them. But seek first his kingdom and his righteousness, and all these things will be given to you as well.
>
> — Matthew 6:32-33

The weight of finding provision is a heavy burden and warps man's perception of life. The lure of wealth, to be free from the painful toil and sweat demands of survival, is what people dream about. Being a millionaire only has meaning by its supposed ability to alleviate the stress and weight of finding provision, allow-

ALL THE ANSWERS YOU NEED TO THRIVE AND STAY ON ASSIGNMENT, ALLOWING YOU TO DISCOVER YOUR PURPOSE, ARE IN THE KINGDOM.

ing us to focus on purpose and assignment. The lottery is extremely popular because it offers provision with no labor attached and an escape from the earth curse financial system. Get-rich-quick schemes abound in every form and continually bombard our emails and Facebook posts. So in the context of our finances, we need to answer a question: Is there a way to go back to that seventh day where everything is complete and intact and available? The answer is a big YES! How that happens and understanding the laws of the Kingdom that will produce that kind of result is the purpose of this book. I know your experience with life or even the church and Christians may argue that what I am saying cannot be true, as so many Christians have embraced the "poverty is holy" theology. But I assure you all the answers you need to thrive and stay on assignment, allowing you to discover your purpose, are in the Kingdom.

> *Blessed are you who are poor, for yours is the kingdom of God.*
> — Luke 6:20

The answer for being poor is the Kingdom! This is the first Scripture that God led me to when He began to teach me Kingdom financial law. Of course, to grasp this concept, you would have to know what is meant by the concept of kingdom, which I have already mentioned. And I think you must have a clear understanding of what actually happened at the Garden when Adam sinned. So let me take a moment for a quick review.

In the beginning, Adam and Eve did not worry about anything; no sickness and no provision issues consumed their thoughts each day. Each day, all they had to think about was their assignment, which was to love God, love each other, and take care of the earth and the Garden that God gave them. Fear was completely absent from their lives. But when Adam committed treason, everything changed of course. As I said, Satan became the god of this world, man was cut off from God, and God was cut off from having legal jurisdiction over man. Adam was shocked into a new reality of how life works. Again, here are the words God brought to Adam after he sinned.

> *Cursed is the ground because of you, through painful toil you will eat of it all the days of your life. It will produce thorns and thistles for you, and you will eat the plants of the field. By the sweat of your brow you will eat your food until you return to the ground.*
>
> — Genesis 3:17

Painful toil, sweat, fear, worry, and a survival mentality is now what consumes Adam and Eve's thoughts. Their purpose, which was the plan God had for them, is now lost in the race and the battle to survive. Adam's awesome assignment, his purpose, is now smothered by the cares of life and the need for provision. He loses sight of who he is. The only purpose he can now see is to survive, which requires constant toil and sweat. Not much has changed from that day to this.

Today, as a pastor, I find that the biggest question people ask me is, "What am I supposed to do with my life?" The reason they ask is because in the earth realm since Adam, the quest for provision is the goal by which everything else is measured. Decisions are usually made on the basis of money and not purpose. Money and the need for it can force people to take jobs they hate. In reality, most people do not have a clue who they really are. Mark this down, "Until you know God, you will never know His design for your life. He is the one who created you."

People are so hungry to find out who they are. In the world they seem to be just a number, but to God they are a very special and unique creation with skills and potential that no one else has. But because they do not know God and, thus, do not know themselves, they look for their value in all the wrong places. They allow the culture to dictate their value by accepting what the culture says. But the image the media portrays and the mirror of the culture are all shifting shadows. By the time you think you are stepping in line with what it calls acceptable, you will find that it has changed and you are already behind.

I can remember being in Paris and walking down the street with Drenda. Paris is, of course, known for fashion; and that year's fashions were all grays and blacks. Every store window was full of only grays and blacks. As I looked down the street, in both directions, I could see hundreds of people walking along. I was shocked to see not one speck of color. Every single person, without exception, was dressed in greys and blacks. There were hundreds and hundreds of people all looking the same. When was the last time someone told you that their favorite color was gray? But that day, the masses were sure their favorite was gray or black.

Because the pressure to find provision is so intense and warps our identity to whatever we think will help us find it and to be accepted, Drenda and I developed a saying that we have been preaching for years: "If you do not fix the money thing, you will never discover your destiny!" Being a slave to survival lends little time to investigate or create many options. The truth is, as I have shared, most of the time people make their decisions around the goal of either finding or hoarding provision. They abandon their passion for a paycheck and their vision for provision. The fact is we have been so pressured by our survival mind-set of painful toil and sweat that we have stopped dreaming. Fear holds our dreams hostage, and the lack of provision holds our dreams imprisoned to the impossible.

I can remember when my dream was to just have enough gas money to get home, let alone something of life-altering significance. In those days, there were no grand visions on my radar. Just paying the monthly rent check took all the imagination I could muster. I will admit it is hard to see past survival when you are hard pressed for food or face immediate pressing financial concerns.

When Adam gave away the Kingdom, a whole new world of death, fear, survival, and panic took over his life. I'm sure all of us know what fear feels like. I can recall countless stories in my own life of panic, shame, and fear as I suffered through nine long years of financial chaos, eventually dealing with panic attacks, and living on antidepressants. Living in the earth curse system of survival has trained all of us toward a negative outlook on life. Some deal with it better than others, but without Christ, this negative mind-set continually tells us we are not good enough.

Have you ever heard someone say, "Don't get your hopes up"? Growing up, if I ever was excited about something that my dad thought was foolish, he would say, "Someday you will grow up." Because of that, I usually did not allow myself to dream about anything except what was determined to be needed by my dad. I believe my dad had been hurt by growing up in an alcoholic home, and this is what he had to do while growing up as well.

To be honest, we have all been professional worriers since we were born. Fear is the common vernacular of the earth realm. If you will stop and think about it, the word *no* has been so engrained in us from the time we were born. "No, you cannot have that." "No, put that back." "No, you cannot go there." "No, you cannot afford that." Eventually, we just stop saying "Yes" to anything except the occasional escape to an activity that numbs our mind to our actual circumstances, like overeating our favorite comfort food.

One study estimates that the average child hears the word *no* or *don't* over 148,000 times while growing up, compared with just a few thousand *yes* messages.[4]

I recently held our annual Provision conference, and on the platform I put a 2017 Ferrari, a car to be admired for sure. The owner of the car attends my church and paid cash for the car, which was close to $400,000. As the attendees all came in, they admired and stared at the car, all looking it over, wanting a closer look. But although they all admired the car, the point I was making by putting it on the platform was not to inspire a lifestyle of material goals but, rather, to teach them a lesson. The people all gathered around the car, all stating they would love to drive it.

I knew the "no" training they had received in the earth curse system of painful toil and sweat was subconsciously shouting, "NO, you will never own a car like that! No, you will never be able to afford that; don't even think about it." Because of the "NO" training they have had, we all have had, most of them there never even considered actually owning a Ferrari because the no mind-set could not see it or receive it. However, if I kept changing out cars every hour, from expensive down to the cheapest, eventually, I would have a car up on the platform that they would think and say, "I like that car; I should get one."

What was the difference? It was all about how they saw themselves, their potential, and the cost of the car. Yes, there could have been a few there that said to themselves, "I will own that car someday," or possibly there were people there that had the money and viewed the car differently. But I am sure that for the masses, owning a car like that was not even in their realm of thinking. The millionaire who paid cash for the car actually has a half dozen Ferraris. To his

[4] "Becoming a Yes Mom," http://www.babyzone.com.

mind-set, it is just a great car. When he saw the car, he envisioned owning it and went about the process of ordering it from Italy, and then having it shipped to his home in the U.S. It was not hard for him to act on his vision because he had the provision. Here is an important key to rest—provision is pro-vision.

Major Key:

Provision Is Pro-vision

Without provision there is no vision; there is only survival. The earth curse system of poverty has stolen our dreams and our futures. I know the Ferrari was a radical illustration but it made my point. The people there did not even allow themselves to dream of owning a car like that because they viewed it as unobtainable. If they did even for a moment allow themselves to dream about owning it, their training in the earth curse system would scream back at them, "What a waste of money!" But what if you had $25 billion cash in your checking account (I am just making a point)? That car would seem so cheap that you would buy one just to use it on the weekends. It is all a matter of perspective, and since the Word of God says every promise of God is, "Yes" and "Amen (so be it)," your perspective needs to change to think like God thinks.

> *For no matter how many promises God has made, they are "Yes" in Christ. And so through him the "Amen" is spoken by us to the glory of God.*
>
> — 2 Corinthians 1:20

According to the dictionary, the definition of perspective is: a particular attitude toward or a way of regarding something; a point of view, attitude, frame of reference, or interpretation. Basically, perspective is really just how you think about something.

Here is a concept I want you to think about. Adam was a prince before he gave in to Satan. So if you saw him after that fall, you would see an impoverished man with a messed up family (Cain, his son, killed his brother, Abel), and you would not really give him a chance at being anyone. But what you did not see was that he had royalty in his veins. Although you did not see him in that capacity, he had actually been created to rule and reign in life. This same truth applies to you also. You cannot just look at yourself based on where you live, what you have, and your present circumstances, and judge your potential. You have to look at your created potential.

I can remember when I was going through some tough circumstances, and I was facing some big issues that looked bigger than me. I was faced with some decisions that would take a lot more money than I had on hand. I felt I knew what God was telling me to do, but I was still just a little timid about jumping into it. The Lord gave me a dream at that time. I was on a horse on top of a hill. I had a sword in my hand. Below me at the bottom of

YOUR PERSPECTIVE NEEDS TO CHANGE TO THINK LIKE GOD THINKS.

the hill were hundreds, if not thousands, of enemy soldiers on horses with their swords raised against me. I was all alone on that hillside and was surely vastly outnumbered. A voice in my dream said these words, "Don't underestimate yourself, Gary!" At that, I raised my sword and began to race my horse down the hill toward the enemy who by now, seeing my charge, was also charging up the hill toward me with their swords raised. As I was galloping toward them, I yelled loudly, "THOR!"

When I woke, I knew it was the Lord speaking to me and encouraging me, but I did not know what the word *Thor* meant. I have a man in my church who has pastored for 30 years and has studied a lot of languages. I asked him if he knew what it meant and he told me he would check into it. He called me the next day and said that Thor meant the son of thunder. I thanked him and was amazed at what the Lord was telling me. To the enemy, I sound like thunder! Unless I tell the devil how weak I am, when I speak, it sounds like thunder (power) to him.

I was preaching our very first Provision Conference in 2010 and was telling this story. As I relayed the story, I concluded with what the Lord told me in the dream, "When the enemy sees you coming, Gary, you sound like thunder. At the moment I said, "It sounds like thunder," a loud clap of thunder filled the air. There was no rain, there had not been any previous thunder, and that was the only clap of thunder that was heard all night. The people that were there that night were shocked. But no one was more overjoyed then I was, as I knew it was the Lord putting His, "AMEN" on what I was saying as it applied to all of His children. By the way, the TV cameras were rolling that night, and if you would like to see that event you can go to this link: https://youtu.be/rtx1XYJGIAg.

So here is a concept that you need to understand.

Slaves do not dream big dreams!

What do slaves dream about? Stopping, that's what. They dream of the 5:00 hour as they keep looking at their watches through the second half of the day, wanting to stop and leave work. They dream of vacation, they dream of retiring, they dream of having money so they can stop. Slaves dream of stopping, not of creating more work! A slavery mind-set or perspective does not invent or create work; it looks for a way out of work. A slave is already overwhelmed and just does not see the potential passing him by every day.

To be the head and not the tail, your mind-set has to change from a slave to an owner and creator. You have to start dreaming again. You need to see past who you think you are, for although you may seem weak in your own eyes, to the devil you sound like thunder. You have royal blood in your bloodstream, and you just need to think and act like it.

I have a friend who is a multimillionaire. He owns many beautiful homes, all on the ocean or on lakes. One day as I was visiting him, we were walking down the harbor walk among the boats. As we passed each one, he would call out the owner to me. I will give you an example of what the conversation sounded like, but I am just making up the names, as I do not remember them. So my friend's conversation sounded like this: "This boat belongs to Billy Smith, who owns Ohio Medical Services. This next boat is owned by John Rogers, who owns Rogers and Rogers, a law firm. This next boat belongs to Ralph Tidewell, who owns that nice shoe store on High Street."

As we walked down the row of boats, and after passing by about 20 of them, I realized that each one of them was owned by someone who owned a business. Not one boat was owned by your ordinary Joe working nine to five as an employee at the local ice cream stand. Now, I am not against working at the local ice cream stand and I am not against being an employee, most of the time anyway. I am just giving you an example of the kinds of people that have wealth.

Please pay careful attention to what I am saying. It is not about the money they have; it is about the mind-set they have. Don't get the cart before the horse. Most people would say, "I wish I had that kind of money." What they should be saying is "I wish I thought like they do!" They have a different perspective of life and of themselves.

The majority of families never reach an income that would be considered an abundant income. A current study says 51% of America's workers make less than $30,000 a year.[5] Over half of our nation makes less than $30,000 a year?! If you are in your twenties and just starting out or you are in a position because you really want to be there, and the money is not on the top of your list then fine, but I know that is not true of over half of our nation. I know they need more money. Trust me, I have been in thousands and thousands of homes over my 36 years in the financial services industry, and I've seen it firsthand.

So why don't they have more income? Before you begin to shout how unfair life is or how you are a victim or some other nonsense, I will submit to you that it is because of two reasons. First, they are trapped under the earth curse system of poverty and do not know of God's Kingdom and His principles of provision. Second, they have stinking negative thinking, also because of the earth curse training they have had, and because they do not see a way out, even though one might be staring them right in the face. Basically, slaves have a slavery mentality, as I have been sharing. They do not see opportunity when they are looking for rest. Let's face it; without real answers, people lose heart.

Let me give you an example that I use in my seminars. Let's say I told you that I could solve all of your money problems in one easy sentence. Get your pencil and paper ready because I will guarantee that this will be your answer. Ready? Okay, here it is: make a net income of $5 million this year. When I say that from the platform, everyone starts to laugh. But why do they laugh? Because they cannot see themselves making that kind of money, nor do they think it is possible that they could make a net income of $5 million a year.

[5] Michael Snyder, "Goodbye Middle Class: 51 Percent of all American Workers Make Less Than 30,000 Dollars A Year," "End of the American Dream," *Washington's Blog*, October 21, 2015, http://www.washingtonsblog.com/2015/10/goodbye-middle-class-51-percent-of-all-american-workers-make-less-than-30000-dollars-a-year.html/.

I then tell them that they will never possess what they cannot see. Then I repeat the exercise, but this time I continually lower the number: $200,000, $100,000, $70,000, or $40,000 a year. Eventually, I tell them, "I will come to a number where you will say, "Okay, easy. I can do that."

Then I tell them another story. Let's say that I am a wealthy businessman in the export business. I want to ship balls to China, and I need some help packing them up to ship. I tell them that I will pay them $500 for each ball they box up. Assuming they can package 200 balls a day, that would earn them about $100,000 a day. I would also like to offer them a one-year contract packing the balls at the same rate. Now, if I told them their answer was to make $5 million net income in 12 months, what would their response be? "Easy, no problem, you can easily make $5 million at that rate."

What was the difference? A plan, that is all. The plan makes all the difference. The God that made you knows the plan, and all you need is to hear it. So it is with the Kingdom of God. When God gave me that dream to start that business and then showed me how to do it, my income had not changed yet—but I was shouting on the inside, "This is easy! My money problems are over; I have the plan!"

> "For I know the plans I have for you," declares the Lord, "plans to prosper you and not to harm you, plans to give you hope and a future."
>
> — Jeremiah 29:11

God has plans to prosper you! Once you discover that God has a plan for your prosperity, the battle is half over! Listen, fixing the money thing is not that complicated. Provision is pro-vision! It really is pretty simple. The answer for no groceries is having groceries. The answer for the need of a bigger house is a bigger house. The answer for a reliable car is owning a reliable car.

I know I am speaking with double talk here, but I drove a broken-down car for years. You could see me coming a mile away because I left a smoke trail wherever I went. I know how stressful car problems can be when you need to get somewhere. I also know what it feels like to walk into a car dealership and pay cash for a new car.

AS A CITIZEN OF THE KINGDOM, YOU HAVE LEGAL RIGHTS, AND EVERY LAW AND PRINCIPLE IS NOW AVAILABLE TO YOU.

Guess what? No more stress, no more worry. Why? Because my need is met and I have peace. I can focus on what I am supposed to be doing instead of dealing with a car crisis.

The fact of the matter is that most people have to deal with real money issues to the point of being under stress most of their lives. They may be working so many hours trying to just get by that they do not have lives. Friend, this is not God's will for your life.

As I said earlier, people abandon their dreams and passions for paychecks at jobs they despise. Slaves usually are not very happy people! Unfortunately, this is where people live, unhappy with where they are in life, disgusted, and hopeless. But in reality, they are only a perspective shift away from freedom or, as I just shared, having a plan.

Let me give you a personal example. Many of you know that I love to hunt and fish, ride bikes and hike, anything outside. I grew up in Ohio in a small farming community in what is known as Plain Township. It was called Plain Township because, as you can imagine, it was flat. Of course, that was good for farmers, but it was not the most inviting landscape. I subscribed to every hunting and fishing magazine I could, *Outdoor Life*, *Sports Afield*, *Field & Stream*, and others. I would read the great stories of fishing and hunting the wild and beautiful mountains out west and the lush green mountains of the Appalachian Valley only an hour to my east. Yet I never visited those areas. I was 40 years old before I saw my first mountain.

Why? I had the money to travel, I had my own car, Interstate I-70 runs right through my hometown, and going west passes right through the Rocky Mountains. But the truth of the matter is I never once thought about going there or even allowed myself to think, "I will go there someday." I admired those places through the glossy images of a magazine but never thought about going. They could have been on the moon as far as I was concerned; it just was not a possibility in my mind. When I was 40 and finally drove out west, I could not believe what I had missed all my life. Now, I have to have a mountain fix at least once a year. Friend, there is more out there than you see right now. You are more than you see right now! There is a different perspective to life that you need to see and experience.

When you begin to understand and learn how the Kingdom of God operates and what the Kingdom of God says you already have, your perspective will change!

> *Consequently, you are no longer foreigners and aliens, but fellow citizens with God's people and also members of God's household.*
> — Ephesians 2:19

As a citizen of the Kingdom, you have legal rights, and every law and principle is now available to you. This was Drenda's and my problem. Although Christians and loving God, we were citizens of God's Kingdom with no knowledge of the laws and principles of the

Kingdom. Because of our limited perspectives the earth curse system gave us, we did not have dreams. But knowledge is power.

For instance, in the courtroom, a signed lease agreement proves you have a legal right to live in your house. The knowledge that there is a signed document and access to justice to ensure your legal right to live in that house provides peace and comfort to you. In the same way, knowledge of what God says and what the Kingdom has for you gives you confidence to lay hold of everything that is legally yours. For instance, what is the farmer's prosperity? Is it money? No. Is it the seed he sows? No. It is the knowledge he possesses of the laws of sowing and reaping. No matter how poor he may be, he knows how to become rich. He simply taps into the laws of the earth realm that God has established. The process of seedtime and harvest can produce for the farmer over and over again.

He understands the laws of harvest and has full confidence in them. He sows thousands of dollars worth of seed into the ground, yet he is not afraid. You will not find a farmer sitting next to his tractor once he has planted his crop weeping for all the money he has thrown into the ground. No, he would not be crying over the cost of the seed. He will be confident of the laws that govern the natural earth realm. Can he tell you how a seed grows? I doubt it, but he can tell you that he is looking for more land to farm. The same is true of you and me. Unless we know the laws of the Kingdom and have confidence in them, we cannot enjoy the lives that God has destined us to live.

One of the most exciting stories we witnessed in those early days took place when I received a phone call from a man I'll call "Don," who was facing some severe financial issues. He had heard that I helped people with their finances.

When I first met Don, he had come to my office very discouraged and in debt. Nothing seemed to be going right in his life at the time. When I sat down and talked to him, I found out he was three to four months behind on his rent and on almost every other bill he had. There were marriage issues—his wife was fed up with their financial situation and had begun to lose respect for Don as he was unable to provide for her and their five children. The fact was Don had lost respect for himself, and he was full of questions.

The job he had then involved selling health insurance across the state of Ohio, but his lack of success was quickly leading him down a disastrous financial path.

Despite all the things going against Don, I saw potential in him. He was willing to learn and willing to work. That powerful combination intrigued me enough to hire him and invest myself in the welfare of his future. In the end, it was an investment that paid huge dividends for both of us.

My fledgling company had just won a trip to Hawaii from one of our vendors, and I felt this would be a great chance to share with Don about the Kingdom of God. Although Don was a Christian, he didn't have the same understanding I did. And although I'd tried on several occasions to share God's principles with him in this area, he just didn't seem to believe what I was saying.

I kept looking for a way to catch Don's attention that would help him realize that he, too, could have success by learning how God's Kingdom worked. However, Don was so discouraged that he had a hard time believing in himself and believing that change could really happen. I knew this Hawaii trip was my chance.

In the weeks before Don and I were to leave, we talked of what we would see and do there. One special interest held Don's attention like none other. He wanted to catch a blue marlin in the beautiful waters of the Pacific Ocean. "Hawaii is the blue marlin capital of the world," Don told me excitedly. "I've always wanted to catch a blue marlin; it's been a dream of mine." For the first time in weeks, I saw a gleam in Don's eyes. Something actually got him excited, and I knew his excitement would open the door to a powerful lesson.

"Don," I said, "did you know that it is possible to know, not hope, but *know* that you will catch a blue marlin in Hawaii by tapping into the Kingdom of God?" Confused but intrigued, Don wanted to know more, and I continued with my explanation about the Kingdom. I quoted Mark 11:24, which says, "*Therefore I tell you, whatever you ask for in prayer, believe that you have received it, and it will be yours.*" For Don, this was almost too good to believe. I took some time to help him understand the Kingdom and how to release his faith. And so, before we left on our trip, he and his wife prayed in agreement and believed that they had received a blue marlin. They also sowed a financial seed into the Kingdom of God toward their harvest. This was something the Holy Spirit had taught me to do when I released my faith for something that I needed.

In the meantime, Don did everything he knew to do to uphold his part of the harvest. He did some research on available boats and prices and finally booked with a captain that he felt good about. Everything was set, and we were all so excited about going to the blue waters of Hawaii.

Sail day arrived, and as we boarded the boat, we elatedly told the captain that today was the day we were going to catch a blue marlin. While he expected us to have a successful day fishing for other sport fish, he assured us the odds were not in our favor for catching a blue marlin that day. With two boats on chartered tours every day for the last four months, his crews had only brought in one blue marlin. This was due largely to the fact that it wasn't marlin season yet since marlin are a migratory fish. Refusing to be discouraged, we respectfully told him that we were going to receive one and continued getting our gear ready.

After six hours of trolling we hadn't had a single strike, and I was getting a bit worried that the lack of action might weaken Don's faith. In my concern I yelled out a question to him. "Don," I yelled from my perch on the bridge above him, "let me ask you a question. When did you receive that blue marlin? When it shows up or when we prayed?" In confidence, Don strongly replied, "Gary, that's simple. I received it when I prayed." I was excited and confident when I heard his reply. It was then that I knew Don had taken my instruction seriously and he was determined to have that marlin.

Minutes later, Don's reel began to sing as it bent seaward and the mates yelled, "Fish on!"

"Don't get too fired up," cautioned the captain. "It's a big fish all right, but it's no blue marlin. Marlins come right to the surface and make tremendous jumps through the air and this fish is staying deep." The minutes wore on as Don continued to wrestle with the fish that had yet to come close enough to the surface to be seen. As tired as Don was, the fish was more so and soon gave up the fight. Don and I weren't surprised as he reeled in that big, beautiful blue marlin, but everyone else on the boat was stunned.

The picture of Don and his fish remains in my office to this day as a testimony to others and a constant reminder to me of the reality of the Kingdom. On the outside, it was just a fish. But to Don, the marlin meant so much more. If the Kingdom worked for the marlin, it would certainly work for everything else he needed in life. For Don, it was just the beginning of realizing the impact the Kingdom of God could have on his life.

I love this story, and I love to see people have real experiences with the Kingdom of God. That is what I want for you as well!

CHAPTER 4
I FOUND A MAJOR KEY OF THE KINGDOM!

All of us have keys of various types for our homes, our cars, and anything we want to protect. The key gives us access to what is protected inside or the authority to utilize the item, such as a car. Living as a Christian for nine long years in financial chaos and hopelessness, I knew something was missing, something was wrong. No one needed to tell me that. What I needed to know was what was wrong and how to fix it.

When the Lord spoke to me when I cried out to him for help, lying across my bed in the broken-down farmhouse, he told me that my problem was that I had never learned how His Kingdom operated. In that one sentence I heard the key, or I should say the source of the key or keys needed—the Kingdom. God was telling me that my answer was in His Kingdom. I had never taken the time to learn how His Kingdom operated, but if I did, I would find my answer. When God spoke to me that day regarding my lack of Kingdom understanding, I really had no idea what He meant by Kingdom. But I heard him loud and clear that if I would learn how His Kingdom operated, I would find the answers I was looking for. So to me, a major key was in that general statement, "You have never taken the time to learn how my Kingdom operates!" Of course, that statement in itself said a lot and was, of course, my first major key to my life being transformed.

> *For to us a child is born, to us a son is given, and the government will be on his shoulders. And he will be called Wonderful Counselor, Mighty God, Everlasting Father, Prince of Peace. Of the increase of his government and peace there will be no end. He will reign on David's throne and over his kingdom, establishing and upholding it with justice and righteousness from that time on and forever. The zeal of the Lord Almighty will accomplish this.*
>
> — Isaiah 9:6-7

Understanding that the Kingdom of God is in fact a kingdom which functions on the basis of government and laws opened my eyes to an understanding of the Kingdom that I had never known before. Knowing that the Kingdom of God was established and is being upheld by justice (the administration of law) and God's righteousness (His laws) showed me that everything that happens in the Kingdom is a result of a law or principle of that Kingdom. I may not be the sharpest knife in the drawer, but I was smart enough to understand that if the Kingdom operated on the basis of laws then I could learn those laws and apply them to my life. As God began to reveal and teach Drenda and me His laws, I began to realize that every story in the Bible held keys that I needed to know in regard to how the Kingdom operated. I began to read every story in the Bible differently: "Why did that happen? Why didn't that happen?" I would read every story with the attitude of, "What principles are revealed in this story? How did that happen?"

I began to call myself a spiritual scientist, and I was thrilled as the Holy Spirit would reveal to me law after law. I was even more thrilled to see that laws I discovered could operate in my own life just like they did in the Bible. People ask me, "Gary, what do you mean by the laws of the Kingdom?" I usually remind them of all the laws they use here in the earth realm—gravity, the laws of physics, and all the laws that govern nature.

A farmer uses these laws whenever he wants; he does not have to pray for them to work. They work every time he chooses to use them. They are available to anyone and everyone that wishes to use them. In the same way, the Kingdom of God operates with laws that can be learned. Since they are laws, they never change, and they can be learned and applied to life in the Kingdom.

By the way, once you come to Christ, you are a citizen of His Kingdom, and all the Kingdom is yours. These laws of the Kingdom can be learned and used by you as well.

AS GOD BEGAN TO REVEAL AND TEACH DRENDA AND ME HIS LAWS, I BEGAN TO REALIZE THAT EVERY STORY IN THE BIBLE HELD KEYS THAT I NEEDED TO KNOW IN REGARD TO HOW THE KINGDOM OPERATED.

"Okay," people will tell me, "I get that part of it, but give me an example of a law in the Kingdom." There are many, many laws. Actually, I have already written about a few, like the law of jurisdiction, the law of faith, and the law of agreement, although I did not come out and label them as such in earlier chapters. Again, there are many laws, and all of these laws can be broken down into function and application, which are the parts we certainly want to focus on. Let me give you a story to help illustrate what I am saying.

I own a plane, a Piper Mirage, that I use to fly to meetings, to meet clients, and to travel in business. I had a trip planned to Colorado to attend a conference and had carefully planned the annual maintenance inspection required by law around that trip. If you do not know it, every plane that flies in the U.S. is required to pass an annual maintenance review once a year. My pilot was to pick up the Mirage and then fly us to our meeting. But the day before he was to pick it up, the shop called and said that they had accidentally broken the front copilot windshield. They were going to replace it free of charge, but the process would add three more days before the plane could fly. That meant Drenda and I had to fly out on a commercial flight to Colorado. No complaint intended, but we always prefer to fly our own plane anywhere we go if we can. We were a little disappointed but made our way to the conference. The plan was that our pilot would pick us up for the return flight to Ohio.

Two days into our conference, a sudden hailstorm hit the area. The hailstones were so big that they damaged the entire area. In some areas, the huge chunks of ice actually went through roofs. Hundreds of cars were damaged beyond repair. Buildings and roofs were damaged. As my pilot came to pick us up, he parked at the same FBO that we would have left the plane with if we had in fact flown it out there at the beginning of the conference. An amazing sight met my eyes. Every plane that was parked exactly where my plane would have been parked if it had been there was totaled. My plane, by the grace of God, was not there and thus was not damaged. An amazing story sure enough, but how did it happen? I mean was it just a coincidence or was the plane not being there a result of a spiritual law that I somehow took advantage of?

Well, I know for a fact that it was a result of a spiritual law that I put in place, which I will share with you in just a bit. Understanding a law allows you to duplicate the results whenever you need to. In this case, I practiced a law that God taught me back in the beginning when God first began training me in His Kingdom laws and operations.

Let me show you the law that God showed me, then I will show you how I applied it. Remember, every story in the Bible is showing you something about the Kingdom and how it works. I call myself a spiritual scientist. As I read the Bible, I am always looking for the laws that caused something or the laws that did not allow something to happen. We find the story that relates to this lesson I want to show you in Mark 6.

> *By this time it was late in the day, so his disciples came to him. "This is a remote place," they said, "and it's already very late. Send the people away so that they can go to the surrounding countryside and villages and buy themselves something to eat."*
>
> *But he answered, "You give them something to eat."*
>
> *They said to him, "That would take eight months of a man's wages! Are we to go and spend that much on bread and give it to them to eat?"*
>
> *"How many loaves do you have?" he asked. "Go and see."*
>
> *When they found out, they said, "Five—and two fish."*
>
> *Then Jesus directed them to have all the people sit down in groups on the green grass. So they sat down in groups of hundreds and fifties. Taking the five loaves and the two fish and looking up to heaven, he gave thanks and broke the loaves. Then he gave them to his disciples to set before the people. He also divided the two fish among them all. They all ate and were satisfied, and the disciples picked up twelve basketfuls of broken pieces of*

bread and fish. The number of the men who had eaten was five thousand.

— Mark 6:35-44

This is a great story and illustration of the Kingdom of God operating. Five loaves and two fish feeding 20,000 people! But you say, "Gary, the Bible says there were only 5,000 men there." Yes, it does, but I can assume that there were women and children there as well. So I am guessing there were maybe around 20,000 people there.

When the disciples come to Jesus about the food issue, Jesus wants to teach them something about the Kingdom so He says, "You feed them." Well, that pretty much shocks them. Where are they to get that kind of food? They respond with an understanding of the only source of provision they know—of labor! They say, "Well that would take eight months of a man's wages!" From their dollars for hours perspective of the painful toil and sweat system of the earth curse, it would be impossible to feed them.

But in the Kingdom, different laws of operation make all things possible. Jesus wants to help them see past the earth curse system and learn a new possibility from the Kingdom of God. Jesus then asks them to see what they have available to feed the crowd. They go and look and then respond that they have found five loaves and two fish but know that would not be enough to be of any help. Jesus then asks them for the bread and fish. Holding them in His hands, He prays over them and blesses them. He then gives them right back to His disciples to hand out to the crowd. Of course you know the rest of the story; all of the 20,000 people there ate until they were full and yet there were still 12 baskets left over.

My questions are: "Why did Jesus ask to have the bread and fish brought to Him before He told them to pass them out? Why didn't

Jesus just go ahead and ask the disciples to pass out the food once they found it? Did they have to have Jesus bless it first?" The correct answer is that Jesus had to bless the bread and fish first. You see, the bread and fish were in the earth realm under the authority and jurisdiction of men when His disciples first found them. In that state, Jesus had no jurisdiction over them. But when the bread and fish were willingly brought to Him, He was able to bless them. The word *bless* means to sanctify or to separate. Now, here is a law of the Kingdom revealed.

When Jesus blessed the bread and fish, the fish and bread changed kingdoms.

Essentially, the jurisdiction over the bread and fish changed. God now had the legal right to multiply the bread and fish for the people.

If Jesus would not have taken the bread and fish and blessed them, they would not have multiplied.

We utilize this same law when we bless our food, although I think most people do not realize what they are actually doing when they pray over their food. But simply put, when we pray over our food, it changes kingdoms, thus allowing God to protect us from any harmful thing we may eat. I need to add a side note here. If we willingly continue to live on junk food and eat things we know are bad for us, we will reap what we sow. But if we would have eaten something dangerous, something that we did not realize would harm us, God's Word would have protected us just like it protected my plane. I am not talking about the ritualistic type of prayer you hear most people pray over their food. But praying in faith, thanking God that He removes sickness from our midst allows us, as citizens of His great Kingdom, to enjoy His promises.

> *And when they drink deadly poison, it will not hurt them at all.*
>
> — Mark 16:18

In today's world, we need the confidence of God's protection to give us rest. There are so many things that can steal our peace on every front, including the food we eat. Trust me, you can be sure that Satan has a plot to steal your health and your ability to be effective against him in the earth realm through food!

We can see another example of bringing our problems, issues, our peace of mind, actually everything in our lives under the Kingdom's jurisdiction in Philippians 4:6-7.

> *Do not be anxious about anything, but in everything, by prayer and petition, with thanksgiving, present your requests to God. And the peace of God, which transcends all understanding, will guard your hearts and your minds in Christ Jesus.*
>
> — Philippians 4:6-7

When we pray about something, it brings that problem or issue under the jurisdiction of the Kingdom of God. If we do not pray about it, God's hands are tied. Thus the Bible says pray without ceasing (1 Thessalonians 5:17) and you have not because you do not ask God (James 4:2).

When I bought my plane and when I buy anything, I pray over it, laying my hands on it, and bringing it under the jurisdiction of the Kingdom of God to accomplish what it was intended for as it serves the Kingdom of God and my assignment. Because of this, my plane is off limits to Satan and his minions. No harm shall come to me in that plane!

About a month ago, I was flying the Mirage from Houston to Ohio after a conference. It was late as we made our way across the dark countryside. Lightning lit the sky at a distance on our right and our left as a storm front was moving across the country as well. The storm front caused us to have to make changes in our course to stay clear of the storm, and because of that, we burned more fuel than we had planned on. So to make sure we made it safely home and to satisfy the FAA regulations in regard to onboard fuel reserves, we decided to stop in Louisville, Kentucky, to pick up some fuel. We landed with about 30 gallons on board, but we had another hour to go and did not want to run short. We pulled into the FBO and asked them to put 20 gallons in each wing tank. That would take us up to 70 gallons, more than enough to fly our remaining distance to Ohio as the Mirage burns about 22 gallons an hour.

As we waited in the FBO, the girl at the counter told us she could go ahead and ring up the 40 gallons. As she said that, the lineman came in with some paperwork regarding the transaction. The girl took it from his hands, stared at it, and then said, "Something is wrong here. The numbers do not match." The lineman said that he put the fuel in and he could fix the numbers later. She said, "Okay," but said until the numbers were fixed, she could not give me a receipt but would have to email it to us. We said, "Fine," and walked out to the plane with the lineman. My pilot asked the lineman to verify that he had indeed put 20 gallons in each side, and he said, "Yes, I put 20 gallons in each side."

So we took off for Ohio, and about 40 minutes into our flight, suddenly, the left tank went dry. We were shocked; how could that happen? A minute later, the right tank went dry. It was midnight on a dark night, and we were at 15,000 feet with no power. What happened? We had just put fuel in. People will say to me, "Doesn't your plane have a fuel gauge?" Of course, but our plane's fuel gauges move up slowly when fueling. If you have ever driven an older Suburban, you would probably understand what I am talking about. Their fuel gauges respond slowly to added fuel.

So in this case, my pilot asked the lineman to his face if he fueled the plane and the amount he had put in. We ourselves had seen him with the fuel truck at the plane putting some fuel in. My pilot did his due diligence, seeing the fuel truck putting fuel in the plane and verbally verifying twice that a total of 40 gallons were put on the plane. Once we verify fuel, we set a digital fuel gauge that tracks our actual fuel burn down to a tenth of a gallon. We thought we had done all we needed to do on our part to be safe.

THERE ARE LAWS IN THE KINGDOM THAT YOU HAVE TO LEARN TO BE EFFECTIVE, SAFE, AND TO HAVE PROVISION HERE IN THE EARTH REALM.

We declared an emergency and had to glide into the Greater Cincinnati airport, which really was not a problem since we were directly over it when the tanks went dry, but it was a bit exciting for sure. As we found out later, it was the first plane the lineman had ever fueled. He had put 2 gallons in each tank, not 20. He did not know how to read the meter. Really? And that is all that national company does is fuel planes—incredible!

What the enemy meant for harm was not really an issue, but it could have been a big issue if we would have run dry anywhere else but at 15,000 feet. But again, the enemy cannot harm me or that plane. To head off another attempt by our adversary, we have since changed some of our procedures when fueling. We now do not leave the airplane for a lineman to fuel without us being right there with him monitoring all fueling stops. The incident could have turned out to be catastrophic if we had been low and slow on approach or in bad weather; but of course, it did not as I have a covenant of protection.

Both of these incidents with my plane regarding the safety of the plane as well as myself, were a result of my covenant, my legal rights in the Kingdom. Of course I could tell you the story of how I got that plane in the first place, but I won't right now. I think you get the point—God is awesome!

There are laws in the Kingdom that you have to learn to be effective, safe, and to have provision here in the earth realm. Satan hates us, but he cannot stop us, praise God. Protection is also rest, no worry, and no fear! It is your legal right.

By the way, the law that I just described and utilized is what I call the law of jurisdiction, just in case you're wondering.

Another Scripture that God gave me in the beginning regarding His Kingdom was Luke 6:20.

> *Blessed are you who are poor, for yours is the kingdom of God.*
>
> — Luke 6:20

Drenda and I began to study what God meant by "the kingdom of God" in this Scripture when the Lord first showed it to us. Again, He showed us that He is a king of a kingdom, which is governed and operates by laws. For instance, let's look to our southern border. Every year, thousands of people try to sneak into the United States. Why? Is it because they do not have beautiful scenery where they live? No, of course not. They are trying to come into the United

States because of the government here. Our government has laws that protect people's rights and affords many freedoms that are not available in other nations: property ownership, the right to own your own business, the right to worship as you please, and free speech. All are not available in many other nations.

We have already talked quite a bit about the Kingdom of God, the foundation of all the keys, principles, and laws that God has given us as citizens. Your knowledge or lack of knowledge of these laws can be the difference between life or death, victory or defeat. After suffering through those nine years of debilitating financial fear and now being free, I cannot emphasize enough how important it is to know what it means to be a citizen of the Kingdom of God and the importance of knowing all the laws and principles that make up that Kingdom.

For thousands of years the earth has existed, yet many of the things we enjoy today were not understood. For instance, I want you to picture what it was like on Christmas Eve in 1906 in Ocean Bluff-Brant Rock, Massachusetts. Something happened that changed the world that day. Reginald Fessenden played *Oh Holy Night* to ships out at sea through a radio wave and read Luke chapter two. This was the world's first radio transmission. Now, we pick up a cell phone and can talk to anyone on the planet without thinking about it.

Or how about January, 1879? Thomas Edison successfully invented the light bulb, and now every nation on earth uses the laws of electricity and the laws that govern physics to see at night.

Or how about December 17, 1903? The Wright brothers successfully flew the first airplane, and now we can climb into a modern jetliner and fly all across the world in a matter of hours. The A380, the largest commercial jetliner, weighing 1.2 million pounds, can fly over 800 people for over 9 hours without refueling at roughly

600 miles per hour across the earth. If people would have seen something like this in the 1800s, they would have fainted at the sight of such a thing. But now, it is as common to us as flipping a switch and turning a light bulb on.

The point I am making is that all of these laws were already here, always here, in the earth realm as far back as man was created. They were always available for man to use; he just did not see them. He saw the birds flying, he saw the lightning, but he still did not understand.

The same is also true regarding Scripture. Religion has set boundaries concerning what the Word of God means. You and I have heard, for years, that those things have all passed away, God does not do miracles anymore. The gifts of the Spirit were just for the apostles, or Paul's thorn was a sickness. In reality, the Word is pretty simple. It means exactly what it says. But the foundation in the Kingdom is the first major key you must have to unlock all the other doors.

Now Here Is Another Major Key:

Laws Don't Change!

Drop a rock and it will fall. How many times will it fall? Every time! The law of gravity ensures that you will get the same answer every time. The same thing is true of the Kingdom of God.

CHAPTER 5
FLYING IS BETTER THAN WALKING

Flying is better than walking! As I wrote this chapter, I was flying home from our summer home in Canada in my own airplane, cruising along at 250 miles an hour at 23,000 feet above the ground. For years, we drove to Canada from our home in Ohio. It was a long and tiring 31 hours to get there. I would have to drive all night long to get there the next day. Yes, there were a few times we broke up the trip into two days getting there, but when you have a two-week vacation and four days are spent driving, you lose too much of your time there. But, wow, I was tired when we got there, and then I had to face that same 31-hour drive back to Ohio.

I have always loved planes and have had my pilot's license since I was 19, but I just never thought of owning a plane. I mean, have you checked out the price of airplanes? But the more I was learning about the Kingdom, I realized that I was the one that was holding back that plane with my, "No" and poverty thinking. I actually have two planes now, one that I fly for fun, my first plane, and then the one I use for travel. As I mentioned in a previous chapter, our "No-training" does not allow for dreams or possibilities. We shut them down before they can get started.

I had never thought of owning a plane before. I just did not see how that could be possible. For years, I rented the planes I flew. But as I studied the laws of the Kingdom and saw story after story in my life demonstrate the Kingdom, I decided that I would believe God for my own plane. I did not have the money for one at the time, but I took out a check, and in the memo section I wrote "for my plane." I listed the exact type of plane I was receiving. My wife and I sowed that check into the Kingdom according to Mark 11:24, believing I received when I prayed. This is what the Lord had shown me to do in the very beginning concerning the Kingdom. I had seen this produce in my life many, many times.

A few weeks later, I was having a routine physical done and the doctor casually said to me, "By chance, do you know of anyone that might be interested in buying an airplane?" I was surprised, as no one had ever asked me that before. "What kind of plane is it?" I asked. He went on to explain what the plane was and told me it was at the local airport if I wanted to take a look at it. Amazingly, it was exactly the kind of plane I had sown for! I went by the airport and looked at it, and it was in great shape. I knew this was my plane. But there was one problem; I did not have the money to buy the plane. I told the doctor that I was very interested in the plane and would get back to him.

A couple of weeks went by and I received a phone call from my brother who worked at my father's restaurant next to a building I owned. I had just taken possession of the building a few months earlier in the late fall. I was planning to turn the building into my office complex for my financial services company. The building did not meet the commercial building codes for the purpose I wanted it for, so I knew I would have to rebuild it. I contacted a builder who drew up the plans, and we signed a contract. However, we decided that we should wait until spring before we began the project due to weather concerns. The rehab would involve a complete rebuild of the building.

The previous owner of the building told me that the water was turned off for the winter, so I never even checked it. The phone call from my brother occurred in late February after a warm spell had begun to melt the winter snow. He told me that my building was ruined as there was water running out of it into the street. He and I knew what that meant—the water had not been turned off as the previous owner had indicated. Sure enough, as I examined the damage, the upstairs bathroom pipes, as well as the downstairs bathroom and kitchen pipes, had all burst and water filled the building. All of the drywall, the ceilings, and the walls had fallen off of the studs.

At first, this may seem like a huge disaster, but my rehab plans called for all of the drywall to be stripped from the walls and new rooms configured. The outside siding was also to be replaced as well. So in reality, the water did not hurt the building at all. Any damage that occurred happened in areas that were going to be completely rebuilt anyway. However, when I bought the building, I put insurance on it. The damage was all covered, and the insurance company wrote me a check—and you guessed it—which paid for my airplane. That plane, a Piper Warrior, is easy to fly, and I fly it often for enjoyment. Every time I fly it, I marvel at how great it is to be flying my paid for airplane. I still own that plane now, and it is going on 20 years.

Although in this story the events that took place were pretty amazing, I do not want to leave you with a wrong perspective of how things work. Things do not always suddenly appear as in this story. God may lead you to an opportunity to make the money to pay for your plane, or you could get a really good deal on one. The mind-set you want to have when you sow into the Kingdom is that God will show you the harvest and a plan to capture it. The second thing is to stay within your developed faith and ability. I have had people think that since God would show them how to pay their car off that they might as well go ahead and sow for one trillion dollars. You do not have faith for a trillion dollars! Start with where you are and begin applying Kingdom law and building your confidence in the laws of the Kingdom and your ability to capture what God shows you.

But here is a point I want you to catch. I was a pilot for over 20 years before I purchased that plane. Do you think the laws of the Kingdom worked 20 years earlier? Of course they did. My understanding, or I should say my lack of understanding, did not allow me to envision owning a plane.

Man has watched birds fly for thousands of years, the law of lift functioned in broad daylight every day for all to see, yet no one saw it. What are you not seeing? Think about it.

One of the Scriptures that God taught me in the early days regarding resting in the provision of the Kingdom was Proverbs 10:22.

> *The Blessing of the Lord brings wealth and he adds no trouble to it.*
>
> — Proverbs 10:22

This Scripture refers back to the Scripture and principle from Genesis 3:17 I shared previously.

> *Cursed is the ground because of you; through painful toil you will eat of it all the days of your life. It will produce thorns and thistles for you, and you will eat the plants of the field. By the sweat of your brow you will eat your food until you return to the ground.*
>
> — Genesis 3:17

When Adam lost the Kingdom, he lost the provision of the Kingdom and was left with his own effort to survive. But as you and I have already found out, we just cannot run fast enough with painful toil and sweat to reach the freedom that we so eagerly long for. But now there is good news!!!! Jesus came to preach good news to the poor!

> *The Spirit of the Sovereign Lord is on me, because the Lord has anointed me to preach good news to the poor.*
> — Isaiah 61:1

Jesus was sent to preach good news to the poor. What would be good news to the poor? Simple, they do not have to be bound to the lack and poverty in the earth curse system of provision. Trust me, after living—or I should say surviving—for nine years with nothing but debt and stress, this Scripture was good news, yet it was perplexing. Did it really mean what it said? Wouldn't it be great if it really meant what it said, that the blessing of the Lord really did somehow bring wealth into our lives? I really needed to know if this was true and then how to implement it. One thing I did understand, however, was that the curse of painful toil and sweat only provided at the survival level—and survival was just not good enough. No one wanted free from this curse more than I did, but yet I had no clue as to how to bring that to pass in my life. I think this is how many Christians live—reading the promises of God yet not knowing how to appropriate and then to manifest them here in their own lives.

As I began to study and as the Lord led me in my understanding of Kingdom principles, I read how Abraham was very wealthy. Stop! What about the earth curse system; how did he overcome that?

> *Abram had become very wealthy in livestock and in silver and gold.*
>
> — Genesis 13:2

He became wealthy—no, the Bible says very wealthy—but how? "Well," you may say, "it was because he was Abraham." No, it wasn't, and here is where you need to grab your Kingdom understanding of law. Laws do not pay attention to who you are. They have no respect of persons. If someone, anyone, jumped off of the Empire State Building without a parachute, no matter how great or small of a person they were, everyone would know the result. The law of gravity will function every time. So how did Abraham prosper in spite of the earth curse? Are there clues in his story that we can find? Part of the answer can be found back in Genesis 12. There, God gave Abram, later to become Abraham, a promise concerning his life and his descendants.

> *The Lord said to Abram, "Leave your country, your people and your father's household and go to the land I will show you. I will make you into a great nation and I will bless you; I will make your name great, and you will be a blessing. I will bless those who bless you, and whoever curses you I will curse; and all the peoples on earth will be blessed through you."*
>
> — Genesis 12:1-3

The promise was contingent upon Abraham believing God and obeying Him, and it took great faith to leave the familiar and not know where he was going.

By faith Abraham, when called to a place he would later receive as his inheritance, obeyed and went, even though he did not know where he was going.

— Hebrews 11:8

So we find that God found legal access into the earth realm through a man who believed him even when it made no sense. Abraham's faith enabled God to bless him personally. But later, because of Abraham's faith, God would also make a covenant with him concerning his heirs. Do not think this strange. Remember, this is how Satan himself gained access into the earth realm in the beginning. Adam, who had the legal jurisdiction over the earth, as recorded in Hebrews 2:7-8, chose to believe Satan rather than God.

Abraham's faith, which opened a legal door for heaven's influence in his life, allowed him to prosper greatly. This prosperity extended down through all of Abraham's heirs. As I studied this further, I went on to read about Joseph, Abraham's great-grandson. I found a great illustration and understanding of the Kingdom and how it works, and specifically, what Proverbs 10:22 actually implies.

To set the stage, Joseph's brothers hated him and sold him into slavery through slave traders that would frequently travel through their area. They took Joseph to Egypt, where he was then sold to Potiphar, a captain in the Egyptian military. It was in the following text that I found a major piece to the puzzle regarding Abraham's ability to prosper to the degree that he did.

Now Joseph had been taken down to Egypt. Potiphar, an Egyptian who was one of Pharaoh's officials, the captain of the guard, bought him from the Ishmaelites who had taken him there. The Lord was with Joseph and he prospered, and he lived in the house of his Egyptian master. When his master saw that the Lord was with him and that the Lord gave him success in everything he did, Joseph found favor in his eyes and became his attendant.

Potiphar put him in charge of his household, and he entrusted to his care everything he owned. From the time he put him in charge of his household and of all that he owned, the Lord blessed the household of the Egyptian because of Joseph. THE BLESSING OF THE LORD WAS ON EVERYTHING POTIPHAR HAD, BOTH IN THE HOUSE AND IN THE FIELD. So he left in Joseph's care everything he had; with Joseph in charge, he did not concern himself with anything except the food he ate.
— Genesis 39:1-6

The text clearly says that it was the Blessing of the Lord that caused Joseph's prosperity. But what was or is the Blessing of the Lord? I noticed that it was "the" Blessing of the Lord, not "a" blessing of the Lord. All of us would say regarding something great that "it was a blessing." But this text is not referring to a general, good thing happening. It is talking about "The Blessing."

I realized that the Blessing of the Lord was, in fact, the covenant made between God and Abraham and his heirs. Specifically the Blessing was the promises given to Abraham in that covenant. A legal agreement has in it the duties and obligations of both parties involved, but it also spells out the benefits to each. In this case, the promises given to Abraham were the benefit side of the agreement. The obligation, to enjoy these benefits, was to follow the Lord's decrees and laws. I also saw clearly that whatever Joseph brought under his legal jurisdiction also came under or enjoyed those same promises or benefits.

Then Proverbs 10:22 was making sense to me. The promises of God given to Abraham as a legal agreement overrode the earth curse system of poverty. The Blessing given to Abraham made it legal for God to bless Abraham and his lineage with the prosperity and influence that God had once wanted man to have. Let's now read Proverbs 10:22 with our understanding written inside of the brackets.

A Major Key:

The Blessing of the Lord [the Promises Given to Abraham] Brings Wealth and He Adds No Sorrow to It.

The phrase "*he adds no sorrow to it*" is referring to the earth curse system of Genesis 3:17—through painful toil and sweat. The Hebrew word for *sorrow* also means hard labor! Do you see it? Man can escape the earth curse limitations of painful toil and sweat through the promises given to Abraham. Oh, I know what you are thinking—"Those promises were given only to Abraham and his seed." Yes, but I need to show you another Scripture, Galatians 3:13-14.

> *Christ redeemed us from the curse of the law by becoming a curse for us, for it is written: "Cursed is everyone who is hung on a tree. "He redeemed us in order that the blessing [promises] given to Abraham might come to the Gentiles through Christ Jesus, so that by faith we might receive the promise of the Spirit.*
>
> — Galatians 3:13–14

Now through faith, we as believers in Jesus Christ participate in the blessing given to Abraham. So what is the blessing given to Abraham? We can find a list of the promises listed in Deuteronomy 28.

> *If you fully obey the Lord your God and carefully follow all his commands I give you today, the Lord your God will set you high above all the nations on earth. All these blessings will come upon you and accompany you if you obey the Lord your God:*
>
> *You will be blessed in the city and blessed in the country. The fruit of your womb will be blessed, and the crops of your land and the young of your livestock—the calves of your herds and the lambs of your flocks.*
>
> *Your basket and your kneading trough will be blessed.*
>
> *You will be blessed when you come in and blessed when you go out.*
>
> *The Lord will grant that the enemies who rise up against you will be defeated before you. They will come at you from one direction but flee from you in seven.*
>
> *The Lord will send a blessing on your barns and on everything you put your hand to. The Lord your God will bless you in the land he is giving you.*
>
> *The Lord will establish you as his holy people, as he promised you on oath, if you keep the commands of the Lord your God and walk in his ways. Then all the peoples on earth will see that you are called by the name of the Lord, and they will fear you. The Lord will grant you abundant prosperity—in the fruit of your womb, the young of your livestock and the crops of your ground—in the land he swore to your forefathers to give you.*
>
> *The Lord will open the heavens, the storehouse of his bounty, to send rain on your land in season and to bless all the work of*

FLYING IS BETTER THAN WALKING

your hands. You will lend to many nations but will borrow from none. The Lord will make you the head, not the tail. If you pay attention to the commands of the Lord your God that I give you this day and carefully follow them, you will always be at the top, never at the bottom. Do not turn aside from any of the commands I give you today, to the right or to the left, following other gods and serving them.

— Deuteronomy 28:1-14

All of these promises, although in the Old Testament, are now yours to enjoy. The difference is that in the Old Testament the people accessed them through what they did, but we access them through our faith in Jesus Christ under the new covenant. You and I, as Gentiles, have been grafted in; and now, through Jesus Christ we share in the Blessing of Abraham. But we have more than just the physical blessing of Abraham, we have the spiritual blessing of the new birth. We now have the physical, earthly blessing of Abraham, but we also have the eternal blessing of heaven and the Holy Spirit actually dwelling in us as sons and daughters of God. Remember, only sons and daughters gain the inheritance; slaves cannot. Without the new birth, although Abraham loved God, the Holy Spirit did not dwell in him, nor could he enter into heaven. Of course, he gained heaven after Jesus paid off the debt of sin.

I now understood what Proverbs 10:22 actually meant when it said that God brings wealth and he adds no sorrow to it. *Sorrow* in the Hebrew language means hard labor, which I understood now to refer to the earth curse system of painful toil and sweat. I understood that this covenant, this blessing of the promise of God's help and His benefits, lifted Abraham above the earth curse and caused him to prosper. I realized that the benefits of that blessing as defined in

91

Deuteronomy 28, clearly showed me that I was to prosper. The effect of these promises would be that I was destined to be the head and not the tail, the lender and not the borrower. This is the legal right of every child of God. Like Joseph, I have the blessing of God, and I should prosper. I also have the inheritance of the entire Kingdom of God. As a son, all of it is already legally mine.

As I looked at the story of Joseph again in Genesis 39, I clearly saw that it was Joseph's success that caught Potiphar's attention, and it was also visible success that was to catch the attention of the nations of the world and let them see a difference in the people of God.

> *Then all the peoples on earth will see that you are called by the name of the Lord, and they will fear you. The Lord will grant you abundant prosperity—in the fruit of your womb, the young of your livestock and the crops of your ground—in the land he swore to your forefathers to give you.*
>
> — Deuteronomy 28:10-11

There was another huge clue in Genesis 39:6 that I also noted and want you to see. Speaking of Potiphar, it says, "*So he left in Joseph's care everything he had; with Joseph in charge, he did not concern [worry] himself with anything except the food he ate.*" I saw it! Here was an example of the rest that we are talking about. Potiphar did not have to worry about anything except the food he ate. This implies that the success that Joseph brought to his household, the Blessing of the Lord, produced results that allowed Potiphar to focus on his assignment and not survival!

Drenda and I have a saying that we have used for years, "Until you fix the money thing, you will never discover your destiny," and will never discover who you really are. You will never find your niche, your passion point, never truly find contentment. You will be making all your decisions around survival, finding or hoarding money, being someone you're not just to make a paycheck. Here we see the effect of the Blessing of the Lord on Potiphar, who did not even know anything about the Kingdom of God. By putting his stuff under Joseph's care, his estate, his concerns were transferred under the covenant that Joseph carried. You can clearly see the moment this transfer happened in verse 5 of chapter 39.

> From *the time* he put him in charge of his household and of all that he owned, the Lord blessed the household of the Egyptian because of Joseph. The blessing of the Lord was on everything Potiphar had, both in the house and in the field.
>
> — Genesis 39:5

Here again we see this transfer of something in the earth realm, which is subject to the earth curse system, coming under the jurisdiction of the Kingdom of God and drastic changes taking place. Let's face it: If God is helping you with His wisdom, leading you to right decisions, and warning you of possible pitfalls, anyone can prosper! Do you see it? The Blessing of the Lord is yours!

As I studied this as the Lord was teaching me about the Kingdom, I was confused as to why Joseph had tremendous success because of this blessing, yet most Christians I know today are struggling to pay their bills. Being completely free financially is something most do not even think possible. Yet, we have a better covenant based on better promises then those of the Old Testament. Although I clearly understood the Blessing of the Lord, I still did not know exactly how that blessing actually produced the answers that I needed—but I was learning and enjoying more and more freedom as I began to apply and experiment with what God was teaching me.

I then turned my attention to the New Testament and looked at Jesus and His ministry to learn more about how the Kingdom of God was changing situations and circumstances there.

> *One day as Jesus was standing by the Lake of Gennesaret, with the people crowding around him and listening to the word of God, he saw at the water's edge two boats, left there by the fishermen, who were washing their nets. He got into one of the boats, the one belonging to Simon, and asked him to put out a little from shore. Then he sat down and taught the people from the boat.*
>
> *When he had finished speaking, he said to Simon, "Put out into deep water, and let down the nets for a catch." Simon answered, "Master, we've worked hard all night and haven't caught anything. But because you say so, I will let down the nets."*
>
> *When they had done so, they caught such a large number of fish that their nets began to break. So they signaled their partners in the other boat to come and help them, and they came and filled both boats so full that they began to sink.*
>
> *When Simon Peter saw this, he fell at Jesus' knees and said, "Go away from me, Lord; I am a sinful man!" For he and all his companions were astonished at the catch of fish they had taken, and so were James and John, the sons of Zebedee, Simon's partners.*
>
> *Then Jesus said to Simon, "Don't be afraid; from now on you will catch men." So they pulled their boats up on shore, left everything and followed him.*
>
> — Luke 5:1–11

Here is a story of how the Kingdom of God reversed the earth curse system in the lives of three fisherman one morning. If you read the text, you find that Peter, James, and John had fished all night long without catching a thing, nothing. Typical of the earth curse system of painful toil and sweat, they came up short for the night with nothing to show for their labor. But when Jesus taps into the Kingdom of God and its function, the same fishermen catch so many fish that their boats almost sink!

Stop!!!! Let's think about what we have just read. Nothing, no fish, broke, turns into a harvest that almost sinks two boats? Yet people read this story and have read this story for hundreds of years and do not see or even think this could still happen for them. Why? The usual response would be that Jesus was there and He did it. Remember the story I showed you in Mark 6 where Jesus could not heal the people because the people were not in faith, and thus, the Kingdom had no jurisdiction? Someone had to give heaven jurisdiction before heaven could act in this situation.

Simon answered, "Master, we've worked hard all night and haven't caught anything. But <u>because you say so, I will let down the nets</u>."

Peter came into agreement with heaven, and heaven had legal access in this story. Again, we see the earth realm transformed by the Kingdom of God. Crazy isn't it, just like people seeing birds fly for thousands of years but not realizing that flight was possible for them and thus never pursuing it. So are Christians today, not realizing that they do not have to put up with empty nets but have access to heaven's power to help them prosper in life. The thing I want you to see here is that the same guys that came up short are the same guys that have two boats so full they are sinking!

My friend, the difference is the Kingdom, not the people. You may think you do not have a future, coming up short, with nothing working out. But in reality, all you need is the Kingdom to turn your life into a success story. Yes, you have your part to play. They had to go out fishing—they had to take care of their nets, and prepare for the catch—but anyone can catch fish if God shows you where.

Listen, the earth curse system of running and sweating cannot get it done. You cannot run fast enough or long enough to capture your dreams. God never intended for you to grit your teeth and try in your own strength to get things done.

By tapping into the laws and the promises of the Kingdom of God, we can fly instead of walk. Let me put it a different way. Although the law of gravity is still in effect, we can fly by tapping into another law, the law of lift, and enjoy a whole new way of living.

Remember, when you come to Christ, you are a member of God's Kingdom. As a citizen, you are inferring legal rights; and as a son or daughter, you are inferring that you have a right to the inheritance. Your legal rights and benefits have set you high above the earth curse system of poverty, disease, and failure.

Imagine what this verse must have sounded like to an Israelite who had been a slave all their lives. In fact, all they knew was slavery as far back as they could remember. These are the words Moses spoke to the nation of Israel as they were heading out to enter the land of promise.

> *When the Lord your God brings you into the land he swore*
> *to your fathers, to Abraham, Isaac and Jacob, to give you—a*

land with large, flourishing cities YOU DID NOT BUILD, houses filled with all kinds of good things you did not provide, wells you did not dig, and vineyards and olive groves you did not plant—then when you eat and are satisfied, be careful that you do not forget the Lord, who brought you out of Egypt [the other kingdom] out of the land of SLAVERY [kingdom of slavery].

— Deuteronomy 6:10-12

As former slaves, the only way they knew of getting something done was the painful toil and sweat way. But here God was telling them that their own labor would not supply what they needed. He was not telling them they would no longer labor at anything, but that they would not be bound to a system that required labor to just survive. God says that they would prosper in the land he was leading them to.

Let me close out this chapter with one more story that further illustrates what I am saying. Drenda and I are not really into cars. Some people are, and they could tell you of all the cars they admire. For some reason, we just never got into cars. Now, don't get me wrong. We like nice things, but we just have never said that we really must have a particular car. We usually buy a car

ALL YOU NEED IS THE KINGDOM TO TURN YOUR LIFE INTO A SUCCESS STORY. YES, YOU HAVE YOUR PART TO PLAY.

then drive it for 10 or so years. Of course, we take good care of our cars and they never look like old cars, but as long as they look good and run great, we are happy.

But a few years ago, we had our church rent a couple of Escalades for a conference we were hosting. We rented them to drive our guests around, and we wanted to provide a nice vehicle to do so. Now, this was not the first time we had done that. We have always done that. But it was the first time we had driven one of them while we had them on the property for an event. I am not sure why we drove one during this particular event, but we drove it home overnight. And do you know what? We loved it. Drenda and I loved how it drove and how it looked.

At the time, we were driving a nice Honda Pilot, but the Escalade was a step above the Pilot for sure. It was the platinum pearl white model and was the shorter version. If you know much about these Escalades, they come in two sizes, the long one and a shorter one. We liked the shorter one better as it seemed to handle better, with a little more agile maneuverability. As I was driving the Escalade with Drenda she said, "You know, I like this; I think we should get one of these." I agreed. "We should get one just like this one, the short version in pearl white." We both agreed.

Although we did not tell anyone about our conversation, about a month later, as I was walking outside to pick up my paper, my cell phone rang. I recognized the voice on the other end of the line as someone who attended my church. He said, "Hello," and then said that he wanted to buy me an Escalade. I was taken aback for a minute but said, "Great!" He then asked me what color I would like, and I told him that we loved the pearl white one. He said, "I will call you back when I get one for you." He did not ask me if I wanted the short one or the long one, however. A month went by and I thought maybe he had forgotten about the car, but sure enough, he called and told us to come by, that he had the Escalade ready for us to pick up.

As we met him, we saw a beautiful pearl white, short version Escalade sitting there. It was perfect in every way, without a scratch, literally perfect. We told him we loved it. He then apologized, saying he was sorry it took so long but although he had tried to find a long version, all he could find was the short one. We laughed and said, "The short one is the one we wanted." We drove that car home and thought we were the richest people on the planet driving that car. But you know what? Those Escalades have been around for a long time. I just never thought to have one! To understand this story completely, you need to know that I have given eight cars away in the past, so I had seed in the ground in regard to cars. I just never said I wanted one.

P.S. – I know what you are thinking, that these kinds of things only happen to preachers. Well, I have been in the financial field for 36 years and have talked to a lot of preachers. To tell you the truth, the majority of them live hand to mouth. No, these things have not and do not happen to us because we preach about the Kingdom, but because we live in the Kingdom and apply the laws of the Kingdom to our lives. In fact, I was out of debt before I ever started my church. I did not need to start my church so I could have a job to pay my bills, just saying. I started my church to tell people what Drenda and I had discovered—the good news of the Kingdom!

CHAPTER 6
THERE IS MORE TO LIFE THAN PAYING THE BILLS!

It seemed like a brief oasis of life in the storm of life I was facing. We had invited about 50 people over to our old farmhouse for an afternoon to enjoy a bonfire, hot dogs, and fellowship. This was during the years of extreme stress with no money, just struggling to survive one more week. I was looking forward to the event as I was emotionally tired and needed something positive to focus on a bit. The evening was a great success: the food was great, many of our friends came with their children, and all were having a good time. The house was packed when there was a knock at the door. I thought it might be a latecomer to our meeting, but as I opened the door, I was greeted by an employee from the electric company. He politely said he was there to turn my power off for the unpaid bill. I was horrified. My house was full of guests and I needed the power on, besides the embarrassment that it would cause.

I quickly asked the employee to step away from the house to the backyard for a minute. I asked him what it would take to keep the lights on and he gave me an amount. "Too high," I thought. "Can you make it a bit lower?" He thought for a minute and finally gave me a lower number. "Can you hold the check until Tuesday before you deposit it?" I asked. He said, "No problem," and I wrote out the check. There was no money in the account on that Friday, and I did not know how any would be there before Tuesday either, but at least the power stayed on throughout the weekend. I do not remember what I did on Tuesday, but I probably found something to pawn.

This was one day in our life living in financial dysfunction. Now envision living this way for nine years! Living under that kind of stress stops all vision and siphons off every ounce of joy a day may bring. Every thought is focused on surviving, where to find the money for the next bill. Did I spend too much last week? Should I take my calculator grocery shopping with me to make sure I do not go over? Always thinking about how to do something the cheapest way possible. Friend, that is not living! Take a look at what Matthew 6:25 says.

> *Therefore I tell you, do not worry about your life, what you will eat or drink; or about your body what you will wear. Is not life more important than food, and the body more important than clothes?*
>
> — Matthew 6:25

Jesus is saying that the things of life are not life! Everything here in life is to support life, our purpose. But since Adam lost the provision of the Kingdom, life flipped upside down and now everything that supports life is more important than life itself. People have no clue what real life even is and they certainly do not know who they really are. Ask anyone who they are and they will tell you what they do. "I am a doctor, I am a Realtor," etc. No, that is not who you are; it is what you do. Man has lost his dreams. What I mean is that man now dreams of how to make more money but has lost the dream of purpose. In other words, whatever is paying the most money becomes his dream. However, because each person is uniquely created with different talents and abilities, they find themselves in an occupation or job that is not their passion. Life becomes long, drawn out weeks waiting for freedom on the weekend, or long drawn out lives waiting to retire.

So let me ask you a question. If you had no need for money, had more money than you could ever spend in your lifetime, what would you do? You would probably come up with something different than what you are doing right now. As I mentioned before, I know from statistics that at least 70% of Americans, when asked if they like their job, said they are not doing what they love. I want you to understand that this running after wealth, this pressure to perform, and the constant worry over tomorrow was never the plan of God in the beginning.

> *So God created mankind in his own image, in the image of God he created him; male and female he created them. God blessed them and said to them, "Be fruitful and increase in number; fill the earth and subdue it. Rule over the fish of the sea and the birds of the air and over every living creature that moves on the ground."*
>
> *Then God said, "I give you every seed-bearing plant on the face of the whole earth and every tree that has fruit with seed in it. They will be yours for food. And to all the beasts of the earth and all the birds of the air and all the creatures that move along the ground—everything that has the breath of life in it—I give every green plant for food." And it was so.*
>
> *God saw all that he had made, and it was very good. And there was evening, and there was morning—the sixth day.*
>
> — Genesis 1:27-31

Man was created on the sixth day of creation—at the end of the sixth day, to be exact. He was created at the end of the sixth day because he was created to dwell with God on the seventh day, the day we know as the day of rest.

> *Thus the heavens and the earth were <u>completed</u> in all their vast array. By the seventh day God had finished the work he had been doing; so on the seventh day he rested from all his work. And God blessed the seventh day and made it holy, because on it he rested from all the work of creating that he had done.*
> — Genesis 2:1-3

The Bible says that God rested on the seventh day. He was not tired! He was finished. Everything was complete. Everything that man would ever have need of on the earth was already on the earth when man showed up. Peace! Man had all the provision he would ever need. There was no worrying about paying the bills, no worrying over being sick. He had a perfect body and a perfect wife. The only thing they would focus on was each other, God, and their assignment, or their purpose. Adam was in charge of the earth; he ruled over it completely by the authority

WEALTH LURES US WITH THE POSSIBLE ESCAPE TO A PLACE OF REST—A PLACE WHERE WE CAN FOCUS ON WHAT WE REALLY WANT TO DO, LIVE LIVES FULL OF PURPOSE INSTEAD OF SURVIVAL.

and power of the Kingdom of God. But we already know how that story ended. Adam and Eve committed treason against the Kingdom of God and lost their position, lost their provision, and lost their purpose. Their purpose became one of survival. Worry and fear now consumed their thoughts and the struggle to survive. As Genesis 3:17 says, it required painful toil and sweat.

Adam lost the seventh day!

There was no rest now, no peace. A dark incompleteness enveloped his life, and Adam had to run to stay ahead of the void. Man has lived in this state of incompleteness ever since. But there was hope. When man fell, God gave him a remembrance, a picture if you will, of what He would someday restore back to His creation. It was called the Sabbath. The word *sabbath* literally means rest. The seventh day of the week was given to man as a Sabbath day. The requirement for the Sabbath, as you can imagine, was to do no work; no sweating and painful toil were allowed. It was a day when man was to stop, enjoy his family, and to worship God. All of the provisions for the Sabbath had to be completed before the Sabbath began. Even the Sabbath meal had to be prepared the night before. It was a day of rest with full provision and every detail of possible need already attended to. Man could stop and think of something other than survival.

The Sabbath day was just that, a day. But man has been dreaming of a life of rest ever since. Man's quest for wealth is a symptom of his desire to be free from the painful toil and sweat that has held him prisoner his entire life. Wealth lures us with the possible escape to a place of rest—a place where we can focus on what we really want to do, live lives full of purpose instead of survival.

Today, the Sabbath, the seventh day, whether you celebrate it on Saturday or Sunday, is not held in high honor in our culture. Yes, most people that do attend church do go on Sunday morning. Yet looking at the culture as a whole, you would not be able to tell it apart from any other workday. When I was a child, everything closed down on Sunday. You could not go shopping on Sunday; you could not even buy gas on Sunday. My father would have to be sure to buy gas on Saturday night to be sure he had what he needed on Sunday. If you know much about me, you know I enjoy hunting, but as a hunter, I could not even hunt on Sunday either. It was illegal to hunt on Sunday. People used to wear their finest clothes and have big family dinners on Sunday. But of course that has all changed today. But the true picture of the Sabbath has not.

But no matter how well the Sabbath was prepared for, no matter how great the family meal, Monday was coming. The phrase "Monday morning blues" has been synonymous with the word *dread* for as long as I can remember. "I have to go to work" and "back to the old grindstone" were phrases that were used to describe Monday morning. And if you stop and think about it, it almost sounded like slavery. But thank God it's Friday! Even today, the weekend and the Sabbath do offer a brief resting place for most people. But it is short lived and the Monday morning traffic jam awaits.

But what if there really was a way to live life in perpetual Sabbath. How awesome it would be if there really was a way to live life free from fear, full of provision, full of purpose, and living in a place of rest! Drenda and I lived a life of torment, fear, sickness, and insecurity for nine long years until we found that the Sabbath rest was in fact an option for our lives. I am serious!

> *There remains, then, a Sabbath-rest for the people of God; for anyone who enters God's rest also rests from his own work, just as God did from his. Let us, therefore, make every effort to enter that rest, so that no one will fall by following their example of disobedience.*
>
> — Hebrews 4:9-11

Friend, this is the New Testament. There is a Sabbath rest available for the people of God today. This Scripture implies that we can enter into God's rest and rest from our work. Remember what we just studied: God's rest says everything is whole, complete, and provision is readily available. There is freedom from the survival mentality, freedom from being imprisoned by poverty, and freedom from sickness and disease. There are new options! The Sabbath was not just Old Testament information, it is for us today as well. But before

HOW AWESOME IT WOULD BE IF THERE REALLY WAS A WAY TO LIVE LIFE FREE FROM FEAR, FULL OF PROVISION, FULL OF PURPOSE, AND LIVING IN A PLACE OF REST!

you think I am talking about living under all the Old Testament legalism and rituals again, I am not. Instead, I want to examine this Sabbath rest that Hebrews talks about. Because as Drenda and I have found out, herein lies a very important key to the Kingdom of God functioning and providing in our lives as God intended.

SHOCKER: THE SABBATH IS NOT A DAY ANY LONGER!

I hope that statement got your attention. There has been great discussion in the body of Christ as to how the Sabbath should be celebrated: Saturday, Sunday, or beginning at sundown on Friday night until sundown on Saturday evening. Whole denominations have been built around their interpretation of the Sabbath. Before you throw this book across the room in disgust thinking I am a heretic, please bear with me for just a moment, and let's take a look at Colossians 2:16–17.

*Therefore do not let anyone judge you by what you eat
or drink, or with regard to a religious festival, a New Moon
celebration or a Sabbath day. These are a shadow of the things
that were to come; the reality, however, is found in Christ.*

— Colossians 2:16–17

Pay close attention to what Paul says. The Sabbath day was a shadow of the things that were to come; the reality, however, is found in Christ. The Sabbath day was a shadow, it was not the real thing. If Christ is the real thing, then the Sabbath day was a shadow of who He is and what He did. Let me say it this way: There is no power in the Sabbath day to take away or change the earth curse system of painful toil and sweat that Adam brought into the earth realm. If you religiously honor it, by itself and of itself, it has no power to set you free. But it is a shadow, a picture, of what you will find in Christ.

When I was in first grade, my teacher had all of us make silhouette drawings of our heads from the side. They took a projector and had us sit in front of it, and it cast a shadow of our heads onto a white piece of paper. They then drew the outline of our shadows and created our silhouettes, which we cut out and took home to our mothers for Mother's Day. The shadow did capture some likeness of me, but it did not capture my essence, my character, or personality. But it did give some information about me.

The Sabbath did the same thing. Its shadow said to not work, no painful toil and sweat. It was only a shadow, however, not the real thing. But it was pointing to Jesus Christ, who has, in fact, set us free from the curse of the law and the earth curse system and reestablished us as sons and daughters of God and citizens of God's great Kingdom! Again, it was a picture of what Jesus would bring back to us someday. It is a finished work where everything we need for life has been restored back to us. However, as Hebrews says, we enter into this rest through faith. Remember, faith is required to make it legal for heaven to have jurisdiction here in the earth realm. On the cross Jesus cried out, "It is finished!" just as God said it was finished at the end of the sixth day.

The Sabbath for most people today is a religious day. People look upon the Sabbath as God's day, a day where we owe it to God to go to church, do stuff for God, and do other religious things. Jesus had to correct His disciples, who had the same mind-set.

> *The Sabbath was made for man, not man for the Sabbath.*
> — Mark 2:27

The Sabbath was made for man, not man for the Sabbath. Do you know a lot of people feel guilty if they miss church? Why would they feel guilty for missing church when, in fact, they are the church? I am not saying we should not assemble together in worship at all, but the mind-set indicates that they have a wrong view of the Sabbath.

I know you may still be confused, so let me go a bit deeper by looking at a comment Jesus said in John 11.

> *On his arrival, Jesus found that Lazarus had already been in the tomb for four days. Bethany was less than two miles from Jerusalem, and many Jews had come to Martha and Mary to comfort them in the loss of their brother. When Martha heard that Jesus was coming, she went out to meet him, but Mary stayed at home.*
>
> *"Lord," Martha said to Jesus, "if you had been here, my brother would not have died. But I know that even now God will give you whatever you ask."*

Jesus said to her, "Your brother will rise again."

Martha answered, "I know he will rise again in the resur-rection at the last day."

Jesus said to her, "<u>I am the resurrection</u> and the life. He who believes in me will live, even though he dies; and whoever lives and believes in me will never die. Do you believe this?"

"Yes, Lord," she replied, "I believe that you are the Christ, the Son of God, who was to come into the world."

— John 11:17-27

Jesus said He was the resurrection; it was not just a day. The Sabbath day was and is a shadow of what Jesus did on the cross for us. Jesus is the true Sabbath and in Him we find access to the Kingdom of God and all that it has. Thus, we can rest!

So let's go back now to our New Testament Scripture in Hebrews.

There remains, then, a Sabbath-rest for the people of God; for anyone who enters God's rest also rests from his own work, just as God did from his. Let us, therefore, make every effort to enter that rest, so that no one will fall by following their example of disobedience.

— Hebrews 4:9-11

The shadow of the Sabbath day says it is forbidden for you to toil and sweat for what you need on the Sabbath day, but it was only giving us a glimpse of what Jesus did, which was freeing us from the earth curse system of having to toil and sweat to survive. In other words, what it pictured became the reality in Christ. In fact, the first message Jesus ever preached was aimed at the Sabbath day. In Isaiah

61, we find the words of His very first sermon, which He preached in Luke 4.

> *The Spirit of the Sovereign Lord is on me, because the Lord has anointed me to proclaim good news to the poor.*
>
> — Isaiah 61:1

By saying that there was a way out of poverty, he was saying there was a way out of the earth curse system of painful toil and sweat. It was this slavery to finding provision that held men prisoners and unable to find rest. But the Sabbath day was not the only picture that God gave His people of what was someday going to be restored. There was also the Sabbath year!

> *At the end of every seven years you must cancel debts. This is how it is to be done: Every creditor shall cancel the loan he has made to his fellow Israelite. He shall not require payment from his fellow Israelite or brother, because the Lord's time for canceling debts has been proclaimed. You may require payment from a foreigner, but you must cancel any debt your brother owes you.*
>
> *However, there should be no poor among you, for in the land the Lord your God is giving you to possess as your inheritance, he will richly bless you, if only you fully obey the Lord your God and are careful to follow all these commands I am giving you today. For the Lord your God will bless you as he has promised, and you will lend to many nations but will borrow from none. You will rule over many nations but none will rule over you.*
>
> — Deuteronomy 15:1-6

Notice that they were to cancel all debts every seven years. Again we see God using the number seven to show that everything is complete. There is no lack; He has provided everything needed for man. Yet if some questioned His wisdom in telling them to forgive debts, He added, **"However, there should be no poor among you, for in the land the Lord your God is giving you to possess as your inheritance, he will richly bless you."** He went on to say that they were to be so blessed that they would become the lenders and not the borrowers. Again we see here that the earth curse system of painful toil and sweat was made null and void by a new law of life which lifted us out of the curse of the law of sin and death.

As on the Sabbath day, they were not to painfully toil and sweat for an entire year; thus, they were not allowed to sow their crops. But then things got a little more tedious. Not only were they to forgive any debt that someone owed them, but also they were not allowed to sow their crops. At this point, someone may say, "Hey, I can survive one day with what is in the fridge, but surviving a whole year without working is a little more difficult."

So here again, the shadow is telling us to forgive our debts. He told them they would not have to use debt because they would have so much that they would be the lender and not the borrower. Debt is a system based on insufficiency, but God is going to completely provide for them so debt is no longer needed. The shadow says, "You are not to plant your crops," referring to a new way of living outside of the earth curse system. Now, all of this is found in Jesus Christ.

But wait, there is more—the biggest picture yet to show God's people what was to come. It was called the Year of Jubilee.

CHAPTER 7
THIS IS IMPOSSIBLE!

What you are about to read is amazing. No, let me rephrase that. You will actually think it is totally impossible. I am talking about the Year of Jubilee, the greatest picture of what Jesus wants to do in your finances written in the Old Testament, yet few people even know or understand what it is saying. We have already talked about the Sabbath day and the Sabbath year, both which are shadows of what we have in Christ, but now we come to the big event, the Year of Jubilee.

Just the name sounds like a celebration, doesn't it? However, in the realm of finances, most people—and when I say most people, sadly, this means most Christians, too—do not have much to celebrate. As I shared, I have been active in the financial field for 36 years now. I have owned multiple companies during that time and worked with tens, if not hundreds, of thousands of people on their personal finances during that same time. So I know what is out there. And I know what is usually behind the shiny new car or the nice big home. It is usually a lot of debt and stress. Hey, I am not knocking having a nice car or a big home. It just costs a lot of money today to live.

And the earth curse system is a survival system that is usually going to fall short of setting people free. Trust me, of all the thousands and thousands of people I have met, most were not bad people.

They were doing the best they could on their own, and they did not know of God's Kingdom or what I am sharing in this book either. Of course, you know that Drenda and I lived the financially stressed out lifestyle for nine long and hard years ourselves until we learned about the Sabbath rest. After living that way for so long, you do not realize how much dysfunction you put up with and think is normal.

Several years ago, God dealt with me about my small thinking and let me know that I should be enjoying the Jubilee, the party, but I wasn't. Yes, I was out of debt; yes, I had seen some amazing things happen; and yes, I was happy and content. But I had stopped dreaming and God knew it, and He wanted me to stretch again, to keep me creating and dreaming. I had gotten a little stale, happy but stale.

As I said, I own a financial services company, and I was invited every year, by one of my vendors, to an event to celebrate the previous year's success. The attendance was usually around 250 of the top associates and executives. It was an all-expenses paid trip to some really great places, but for the top few, there was special recognition and bonus checks. Because I was busy pastoring a large church, doing TV, and running my company, I always felt that I just did not have time to do the production needed to reach the upper recognition level.

But one particular year, as I sat in the meeting and watched the top 10 associates get recognized and receive their $100,000 bonus checks, I was convicted. I thought, "Wait a minute! I should be up there on that stage being recognized as well. I am a child of God and the Holy Spirit is my Counselor. I should be up there sharing and demonstrating the goodness of God!" So Drenda and I made up our minds right then and there that we would be up on that stage the next year. How? We had no idea.

For the previous 10 years, I had been doing about $3 to $4 million a year with this one company, but the production required to achieve the top 10 would be around $11 million. I had no idea how I was going to reach that level and was not even sure it was possible with my schedule. One thing I had learned though was I could not get it done in my own strength. So Drenda and I prayed and set our goal, sowing a financial seed, releasing our faith, and calling it done.

To make a long story short, in January of the next year, as the new year was just getting started, God showed me how to reach my goal in a dream. He showed me exactly what I needed to do; and as long as I did what he had shown me, I would reach it. Do you know that we made that $11 million goal that year by one sale! What a thrill it was to be up on that stage at the next convention with the top 10 in the company and receive that $100,000 bonus. Do you want to know how great that felt? It was just a huge party. Not only had we reached our goal with the bonus, but also our income had climbed by hundreds of thousands of dollars that year. Sounds like a party to me!

YOU DO NOT REALIZE HOW MUCH DYSFUNCTION YOU PUT UP WITH AND THINK IS NORMAL.

So when I start talking about some Old Testament event like the Year of Jubilee, don't be nodding off and thinking this is boring stuff because it is not. Remember, life goes better with a party, so let's take a look at the biggest event/party that Israel celebrated and learn how to have your own.

The Year of Jubilee

> *Count off seven sabbaths of years—seven times seven years—so that the seven sabbaths of years amount to a period of forty-nine years. Then have the trumpet sounded everywhere on the tenth day of the seventh month; on the Day of Atonement sound*

the trumpet throughout your land. Consecrate the fiftieth year and proclaim liberty throughout the land to all its inhabitants. It shall be a jubilee for you; each one of you is to return to his family property and each to his own clan. The fiftieth year shall be a jubilee for you; do not sow and do not reap what grows of itself or harvest the untended vines. For it is a jubilee and is to be holy for you; eat only what is taken directly from the fields. In this Year of Jubilee everyone is to return to his own property.

— Leviticus 25:8-13

As I start to discuss the Year of Jubilee, let me lay some groundwork that you should have already noticed. The Year of Jubilee happened every 50 years, and it happened right after a Sabbath year, the forty-ninth year. I think you can already see a huge problem emerging, can't you? During the Sabbath year, the Israelites were not allowed to plant their crops. The Year of Jubilee following that year had the same requirement to not plant crops. So in essence, Israel did not have a harvest for two years in a row then had to wait during the third year for those crops to mature and be harvested before they could replenish their food supply. This could be a serious problem for anyone who enjoyed eating a good meal or was making a living selling grain. When Moses relayed the instructions concerning the Year of Jubilee, you can imagine the confusion it must have caused. Of course, the thought of having three years off was a nice idea, but someone had to pay for it. The first thing they asked Moses when they heard about it was, "How is that possible?"

You may ask, "What will we eat in the seventh year if we do not plant or harvest our crops?" I will send you such a blessing in the sixth year that the land will yield enough for three years.

While you plant during the eighth year, you will eat from the old crop and will continue to eat from it until the harvest of the ninth year comes in.

— Leviticus 25:20–22

God answered them with an amazing answer that we are going to spend a lot of time exploring in the remaining portion of this book. He said that He was going to send such a blessing in the sixth year that it would yield enough to last the three years until the new harvest would came in after the Year of Jubilee. There is a parallel here regarding the days of creation. The Bible says that God was finished on the sixth day of creation and rested. Although He rested, He was not tired. Rather, He was finished. Everything that man needed was created and available to him.

God was now showing Israel a picture of more than enough, which stands in stark contrast to the earth curse system of painful toil and sweat. He wanted them to see Him as their provider and to understand that He provides with a mighty provision. Again, although this was a picture to them of God's provision in their own day, it was not until Jesus came that we see what the shadow was showing us. In the natural, there was just no way to survive those three years without sowing a crop. Likewise, in the natural, living under the earth curse system, there would be no way to win financially without spending your days and nights sweating it out. You just can't run fast enough to get it done. Try taking three years off from your current job while you have outstanding obligations, and you will be mixing a sure recipe for bankruptcy. But God is trying to show them a picture of a new way, one where He provides for His people, just as Adam was provided for by all God had prepared for him during creation.

There are two more things that the Year of Jubilee shows us that we need to see. Again we see the land resting, no toiling and sweating during this fiftieth year. You will also notice that all land was to be returned to its original owner. When Israel crossed over the Jordan River, each tribe and each family was given land by which they would own and produce the food and revenue they needed to survive. In essence, land was their wealth. On it they grew crops and raised their livestock. So to have all the land given back to its original owner was giving back the ability to have prosperity.

Again, this is a shadow of what Jesus did for us. The shadow says that prosperity was to be returned to the citizens of the nation of Israel. The reality says to us the same thing, that our prosperity has been returned to us as well, that the inheritance of God's Kingdom is ours again.

ONCE YOU LEARN WHAT THE SABBATH IS ACTUALLY SHOWING US, HUGE CHANGES CAN OCCUR IN YOUR FINANCIAL LIFE.

There is a third thing the Year of Jubilee shows us, and that is that all slaves were to be set free and returned to their families. This is huge. Again, the shadow says that you are no longer a slave but a son or daughter. The reality in Christ says that you are no longer a slave but a son or daughter in God's house with full rights to the inheritance and the prosperity of the house.

So think about what you have just learned. Jesus gave us back what Adam lost. Jesus set us free from slavery, making us sons and daughters of God. He freed us from the earth curse system of painful toil and sweat, allowing God to bless the work of our hands in a mighty way. Although Jesus paid for all these things, we still must know how to appropriate these benefits into our actual lives here in the earth realm. This is where many, many Christians miss it. Not knowing the Kingdom operates by laws, not knowing their legal rights as sons and daughters and citizens, they believe that God arbitrarily chooses who He wants to bless. Therefore, they do not study the laws of the Kingdom, which hold the keys to actually enjoying and implementing what the Bible says is theirs. I am telling you, once you learn what the Sabbath is actually showing us, huge changes can occur in your financial life.

A gentleman in my church began to hear me teach along the lines of faith and how the Kingdom of God operates. His family and his children studied these laws together as a family. As the new year approached, they decided that they would exercise their legal rights and believe to pay off two rental properties that they had just acquired that year. If I remember right, I think the total needed to pay off both homes was around $400,000. So they prayed and sowed a significant financial seed toward this goal of paying off both houses in that year. This was a huge stretch for them, but this gentleman worked in a field where the possibility existed to find enough clients and/or large client contracts that could fund such a possibility. The family all prayed together and agreed this would come to pass. Each week, the family would review their goal and review the Scriptures that gave them the legal ground to stand on to expect such a harvest. Of course, this gentleman knew he had to do his part.

Well as the year proceeded, sure enough, a few big contracts became a possibility, but with all large corporations, multimillion dollar deals are not brought to fruition quickly. About halfway through the year, this gentleman located and captured a large sale for his company, so large that it accounted for about 40% of his company's entire production for the year. With that commission check, he was able to pay off one of the rental properties. Toward the end of the year, another corporation indicated that they would indeed sign contracts for the multimillion dollar contract my friend was offering them as well. But the date to close on the deal kept moving. The paperwork would be prepared, then the date moved and the paperwork would have to be redone, and then the date would be moved again. It was now late fall when my friend was told that the management team he had been working with had been changed and a new team would be stepping in and taking over.

My friend was floored; he knew what this meant. The incoming management team was not aware of the pending contract, which of course, was now null and void. He would have to start the process all over from the beginning with the new team. As he met the new management team, they seemed favorable to looking at his company's suggestions. After reviewing it in late November, they said they wanted to move forward with it. But again, paperwork was delayed and rewritten until it was two days before the new year. My friend received a call that they wanted to meet and sign the paperwork, and they would be paying with cash if he could meet them and sign it that day. My friend made enough commission on that deal to reach his goal of paying both houses off in the year he and his family had set their faith toward.

It was only by studying the Kingdom principles that even allowed or prompted him to imagine such a lofty goal, as he had never landed such a large account before or made as much money in any previous year that would have indicated that his goal was probable. He did tell me that they had quite the party to celebrate that victory!

Another, "that really happened" story happened with one of my children. Of course, all my kids have watched the Kingdom functioning their entire lives. They have all applied the principles I am discussing and have seen God do amazing things. Although they are in their twenties, they all have their cars paid for; and most of them have their houses paid for or almost paid for. My oldest son, Tim, wanted to buy a house with cash. So he sowed his seed, believing God for a great deal on a home in his price range. He also is very handy with construction, so he was not afraid to buy a fixer upper.

He spent his time looking at homes but not finding the perfect match. But one day, he was driving around and spotted this home that was for sale that he had not seen before. It was a foreclosure, and as he looked at it, he knew the home needed some work, but it seemed perfect. He called the real estate agent and had her check on the price of the home. He could not believe his ears—$37,000. "But how could that be?" he thought.

The agent researched the house and told an amazing story. The house was indeed a foreclosure, and it was listed for $110,000 about six months earlier. That was the foreclosure price, but the home had actually sold for $160,000 a few years earlier. Apparently, no one had shown an interest in the house for the last six months since it had been listed. The bank then kept lowering the price, not knowing why no one had shown an interest. But then as Tim and his real estate agent dug a little deeper, they saw why there was no interest in the house. It was listed in a completely different city with a different address, and even the phone number to inquire was also wrong. So no one knew the house was there! The house, being on a small road in the country, on a dead-end street saw no traffic. The price just kept being lowered until the day that Tim spotted it. Amazing. I told Tim that the house was hidden just for him! He repainted it and did a couple of things to the house and sold it for $160,000.

My daughter Amy leads worship at Faith Life Church. She and Jason needed a bigger home as their family was growing from four to five. Prices were out of sight in the summer of 2017 here in Ohio, and houses that were listed usually were selling within a week. Their hope of finding a home that was large enough in the $250,000 to under $300,000 price range, with 5 to 10 acres of land, and a wish list possibility of water on the property just could not be found. Ranches in the area on 1 acre were going for more than $200,000 that summer. After running around looking at many homes, they stopped looking and prayed. Sowing a seed for direction, they told the Lord, "We are too busy to keep looking like this. You know where our house is, and we are asking you to show it to us at the right time. We are not going to look online, or talk to our real estate agent any more about this house!

But one night, an interesting thing happened. Their daughter, who was four years old at the time, said as they pulled into their home, "Mommy, it is time to move." "What do you mean?" asked Amy. "It's time to move to the house with the big staircase that goes up to my room," said her four-year-old. "What house? Did you have a dream?" asked Amy. Her daughter said yes, she had. Well, that night after they put the two kids to bed, Amy could not shake the conversation and told Jason that maybe they should look online.

Yes, there was in fact a foreclosure that had just been listed, a two-story with 10 acres and a lake in front of it. The price, however, was $26,000 over the $300,000 price range they had sowed for. They reasoned that they could always offer lower, so they called their real estate agent. Their agent was leaving for Florida the next day but could possibly show them the home if they did it first thing in the morning around 9:00 a.m. Jason and Amy said they would meet her there.

The agent was late getting out to the home, but the house seemed perfect. Along with all the square footage in the home, the 10 acres of land, and the lake out front, everything seemed perfect. The bonus was that there were woods surrounding the entire property; it was breathtaking. As they walked into the home, their daughter squealed as she ran up the huge spiral staircase straight to her room. To make a long story short, Jason and Amy said they would like to make an offer. As the agent checked on the home details, she discovered that all offers had to be in by noon that morning. That was less than an hour away! If their four-year-old had not told them the dream, and if they had not checked online that night, the house would have been gone.

They offered the asking price of $326,000 and got the bid. They were so excited. During the inspection, although the roof was in decent shape, the inspector said it would need replaced in 5 years or so. Jason had an idea. He decided to ask the bank for a lower price due to the roof needing work down the road. Their agent told them to not even try, that the house was being offered "as is" and she had never seen a bank reduce the price on a foreclosure due to defects in the home. But Jason and Amy felt in their spirits to write a letter and ask the bank for a reduction. You guessed it, the bank gave them the house for $296,000, less than the $300,000 they were believing God to spend. God brought the house just as they had asked Him to do. When they asked the appraiser what he thought the home was worth, he said, "$500,000." My friend, that is the double portion!

As you can see, my kids are all enjoying the Kingdom way of living. In fact, my youngest, Kirsten, just paid cash for her first house this year at the ripe old age of 20. How? They all know how to go about it the Kingdom way!

CHAPTER 8
THE DOUBLE PORTION

Now, I want to dig a little deeper into how the Sabbath rest actually works and how it is possible to tap into it for your own life. I want to go back to our story of the Year of Jubilee and look at our text. There we find God's answer to the people when they asked how they were to live with no harvest for three years. Good question!

> You may ask, "What will we eat in the seventh year if we do not plant or harvest our crops?" I will send you such a blessing in the sixth year that the land will yield enough for three years. While you plant during the eighth year, you will eat from the old crop and will continue to eat from it until the harvest of the ninth year comes in.
>
> — Leviticus 25:20-22

We see in this text that the Year of Jubilee, as well as the Sabbath year preceding it, were both possible because of the huge harvest that occurred in the sixth year, in this case the forty-eighth year (from the last Jubilee). Without that huge harvest, the Sabbath rest would not be possible. Let's take a look at another passage that I believe will clarify this even further.

Each morning everyone gathered as much as he needed, and when the sun grew hot, it melted away. On the sixth day, they gathered twice as much—two omers for each person—and the leaders of the community came and reported this to Moses. He said to them, "This is what the Lord commanded: 'Tomorrow is to be a day of rest, a holy Sabbath to the Lord. So bake what you want to bake and boil what you want to boil. Save whatever is left and keep it until morning.'"

So they saved it until morning, as Moses commanded, and it did not stink or get maggots in it. "Eat it today," Moses said, "because today is a Sabbath to the Lord. You will not find any of it on the ground today. Six days you are to gather it, but on the seventh day, the Sabbath, there will not be any."

Nevertheless, some of the people went out on the seventh day to gather it, but they found none. Then the Lord said to Moses, "How long will you refuse to keep my commands and my instructions? <u>Bear in mind that the Lord has given you the Sabbath; that is why on the sixth day he gives you bread for two days.</u> Everyone is to stay where he is on the seventh day; no one is to go out." So the people rested on the seventh day.

— Exodus 16:21-30 (the manna)

This passage is, of course, talking about the manna that fell from heaven each day to feed the people and describes that it would not be showing up on the seventh day, the Sabbath. They could not save it from day to day, as it would rot very quickly. Only on the sixth day could they gather it and keep it overnight without it spoiling. An interesting side note concerning why the manna would spoil very quickly each day is found in **Deuteronomy 8:16**.

He gave you manna to eat in the desert, something your fathers had never known, to humble and to test you so that in the end it might go well with you.

God was training the nation to look to Him each day for their food, of course, but for everything in their lives as well. God knew they were heading into more than just needing food; they would soon face walled cities and giants. Their steadfast reliance on Him in that kind of situation would be the difference between life and death.

Let's go back to **Exodus 16:29**. Here, you can clearly see that the Sabbath rest was only possible from the double portion that was given to them on the sixth day.

Bear in mind that the Lord has given you the Sabbath; that is why on the sixth day he gives you bread for two days. Everyone is to stay where he is on the seventh day; no one is to go out.

Do you see it? The Sabbath rest was only made possible by the double portion. This is so important that I am going to ask you to write this down.

THE SABBATH REST IS IMPOSSIBLE WITHOUT THE DOUBLE PORTION!

Let me put it in a different context. Unless you have more than enough, you will never have rest from the running and sweating of the earth curse system. As Drenda and I tell people everywhere we go, "Unless you fix the money thing, you will never discover your destiny!" Why? Because without more than enough, you will not have options and you will be a slave to survival your entire life.

Remember when we read the benefits of the Blessing of Abraham out of Deuteronomy 28:11-13 in an earlier chapter. There we clearly saw that living a life of survival is not your destiny! Just in case you forgot, let's review it one more time.

> *The Lord will grant you abundant prosperity—in the fruit of your womb, the young of your livestock and the crops of your ground—in the land he swore to your forefathers to give you.*
>
> *The Lord will open the heavens, the storehouse of his bounty, to send rain on your land in season and to bless all the work of your hands. You will lend to many nations but will borrow from none. The Lord will make you the head, not the tail. If you pay attention to the commands of the Lord your God that I give you this day and carefully follow them, you will always be at the top, never at the bottom.*
>
> — Deuteronomy 28:11-13

Poverty, survival, and bankruptcy are not your destiny. You are to be the lender and not the borrower, the head and not the tail! This abundance is what the Kingdom looks like. This is the Sabbath rest, more than enough, the double portion!

I know what you are thinking, "Boy, that sure would be nice, Gary, but my life looks nothing like that right now." That's all right, we are not looking backwards, but we are looking to what God says and expecting what the Kingdom says about us. Without the proper picture, knowing what our lives are supposed to be like, we will fall for the tricks and traps and the perverted thinking of the earth curse system. Faith is staying in agreement with what God says, not with our circumstances.

Before I share with you how God taught Drenda and me about the double portion, I want to share with you a story which I believe is the greatest story of the double portion in the New Testament.

The story I want to share with you is one you have heard before many times, but probably not in the context of the double portion or with the Kingdom understanding you now have. We find the story in Luke 15, the story of the Prodigal Son. Again, stay with me here. I know you have read it before, but let's go through it together with fresh insight.

> **FAITH IS STAYING IN AGREEMENT WITH WHAT GOD SAYS, NOT WITH OUR CIRCUMSTANCES.**

Jesus continued: "There was a man who had two sons. The younger one said to his father, 'Father, give me my share of the estate.' So he divided his property between them. Not long after that, the younger son got together all he had, set off for a distant country and there squandered his wealth in wild living. After he had spent everything, there was a severe famine in that whole country, and he began to be in need. So he went and hired himself out to a citizen of that country, who sent him to his fields to feed pigs. He longed to fill his stomach with the pods that the pigs were eating, but no one gave him anything.

When he came to his senses, he said, 'How many of my father's hired men have food to spare, and here I am starving to death! I will set out and go back to my father and say to him: 'Father, I have sinned against heaven and against you. I am no longer worthy to be called your son; make me like one of your hired men.' So he got up and went to his father.

But while he was still a long way off, his father saw him and was filled with compassion for him; he ran to his son, threw his arms around him and kissed him. The son said to him, 'Father, I have sinned against heaven and against you. I am no longer worthy to be called your son.'

But the father said to his servants, 'Quick! Bring the best robe and put it on him. Put a ring on his finger and sandals on his feet. Bring the fattened calf and kill it. Let's have a feast and celebrate. For this son of mine was dead and is alive again; he was lost and is found.' So they began to celebrate.

Meanwhile, the older son was in the field. When he came near the house, he heard music and dancing. So he called one of the servants and asked him what was going on. 'Your brother has come,' he replied, 'and your father has killed the fattened calf because he has him back safe and sound.'

The older brother became angry and refused to go in. So his father went out and pleaded with him. But he answered his father, 'Look! All these years I've been slaving for you and never disobeyed your orders. Yet you never gave me even a young goat so I could celebrate with my friends. But when this son of yours who has squandered your property with prostitutes comes home, you kill the fattened calf for him!'

'My son,' the father said, 'you are always with me, and everything I have is yours. But we had to celebrate and be glad, because this brother of yours was dead and is alive again; he was lost and is found.'"

— Luke 15:11-32

In this story, we see that the younger son leaves home with his share of the estate. This is an important detail of the story as it is referring to his share of his inheritance. So make a note that this younger son has already received his share of his inheritance; he can make no further claim on the estate.

> *The younger one said to his father, "Father, give me my share of the estate." So he divided his property between them.*

Next, the story tells us where this young son went: to a distant country. It is important that you understand that the young son left his father's house, implying he left behind his provision, his protection, and the laws of the nation his father's house resided in. He went to a distant nation, one with different laws and a different way of life. I am sure that this young son really had no idea what he was doing. He enjoyed the benefit of being a son while living in his father's house. All that his father had was available to him while he was living there. But for some reason, he felt that he was missing something, that he was being cheated out of some opportunity that lay elsewhere.

If you have not figured it out already, in reality, Jesus is telling us the story of mankind, the story of Adam. Adam is the younger son in the story who left his Father's house. Adam was the one that felt he had a better future somewhere else than to continue serving God, his Father. I know what you are thinking, "Well then, if Adam is the younger son, who is the older son in the story that stayed?" I will address that question at this end of this discussion, but for now, just remember that Adam is the younger son who left.

Although they had everything, Adam and Eve were deceived into believing there was more somewhere else than to stay in their Father's house. When Adam rebelled against his father's house and chose to leave, he came under a new government, a new kingdom with new laws of operation. The Bible calls it the kingdom of darkness, which is ruled by Satan. I am sure that Adam was shocked by the poverty and hopelessness of this new kingdom. At first, everything seemed great. As long as his money held out, it was just one great big party! But by the time he realized that he made a mistake, it was too late. Then, with his inheritance wasted, he found himself lost. His mind, which was once so full of vision, then focused on the daily task of staying alive. There would be no more tomorrow. It always would be today and today has no promises.

> *Not long after that, the younger son got together all he had, set off for a distant country and there squandered his wealth in wild living.*

The younger son now finds himself in a kingdom that is totally and absolutely bankrupt, a kingdom that exists in a perpetual state of severe famine. The son tries to come to grips with what he is seeing—people are dying of hunger. Coming from a home of such abundance, his mind has a hard time contemplating what he sees. But the hunger pains in his stomach remind him that what he sees is real. To survive, he now forces himself to beg on the streets. In this kingdom of darkness, the earth yields only thorns and thistles, and for it to produce at all, painful toil and sweat must be exerted. Being in great need, the son begs for someone to help him. But everyone is in the same boat. No one is going to give him much because they are all experiencing the same severe famine that he is.

A defining moment happens here for the young son, a shift that has affected both you and me and all of mankind. For the first time in his entire existence, the younger son begs to be paid as a servant, a hireling, doing manual labor. This is a total perversion of his true identity and of who he really is. He is no longer the son of a very prestigious man of honor and wealth, he is the janitor, or the butcher, or the real estate agent, or the mailman, and the list could go on and on. He is now known for what he does and not for who he is! He has lost his identity! To accentuate the loss of his identity even further, Jesus says that he became so desperate that he took a job feeding hogs. Hogs were considered unclean to the Jews, and Jesus tells the crowd that this young son has now become so desperate that he has lost sight of any purpose his life may have had. He now lives a life of shame and disgrace. The royalty he once enjoyed is now a distant memory.

> *After he had spent everything, there was a severe famine in that whole country, and he began to be in need. So he went and hired himself out to a citizen of that country, who sent him to his fields to feed pigs. He longed to fill his stomach with the pods that the pigs were eating, but no one gave him anything.*

I hope you are seeing the parallel between the story and mankind today. When two men meet each other, what do they say? "What do you do for a living?" or "Where do you work?" or "What do you do?" When you ask someone who they are, they usually will tell you what they do. Why? Because in the earth curse system, we have all lost our identities, and we are desperately trying to find them. We copy anyone that attracts attention and seems to have importance. This all came from Adam's decision to leave his Father's house. In our survival mind-sets, we have lost sight of who we really are. But be encouraged, this young son in our story did not stay in the pigpen; and as we follow the story, I hope you find out that you do not need to stay there either.

The Bible says one day this young son comes to his senses and remembers his father's house where even the servants have more than they can eat. I can imagine in his state of extreme hunger he had memories of all the great meals he had once enjoyed. My uncle Harold was a radio navigator on a B-17 during World War II. He came from a farming community and from a farming family. Every Sunday, his mother would serve a big meal of fried chicken, mashed potatoes, homemade bread, green beans, and many other tasty vegetables. Of course, there was always homemade pie or cake for dessert. I know firsthand just how awesome those meals were as his mother was my grandmother.

My uncle's plane was shot down over Germany during the war, and he spent many months in a German prison camp. Food was almost nonexistent. One day, I asked my uncle how he had survived those days, and he told me that all he could think about was getting home to his mother's fried chicken and mashed potatoes. I am sure that this younger son had a similar experience and realized just what he was missing. But he had no further claim on the estate, having already received everything his father's estate owed him. So he thought of a plan. He would go home and beg his father to hire him as a servant. In his mind, working as a hired hand, a hireling, was his only option.

> *When he came to his senses, he said, "How many of my father's hired servants have food to spare, and here I am starving to death! I will set out and go back to my father and say to him: Father, I have sinned against heaven and against you. I am no longer worthy to be called your son; make me like one of your hired servants." So he got up and went to his father.*

So he heads back home with his plan and to plead with his father for a chance to at least work in exchange for a place to sleep and food to eat. But the Bible tells an amazing outcome to this story. As he nears his home, his father sees him at a distance and runs out to meet him with a great big hug. From this point on, the story should be called the story of the Father's love because that father hugged him even though he was covered in hog manure. In so doing, Jesus's Jewish audience knew that hug would make the father spiritually unclean. But this father willingly became unclean on behalf of his son. He then calls for the best robe he has and places it over his son to cover his filth. He took the signet ring representing his own authority and placed it back on his son's finger. He gives him sandals to wear, which implies he again has access to the entire estate. But it is the last item his father gives him that causes the older son to become furious. The father calls for the fatted calf to be killed and served on behalf of the son's return. The younger son, although undeserving, is given back the position and benefits of being a son, openly and freely honored as a son, and completely restored to his former position as a son in the house.

Okay, what does all this have to do with the double portion? Everything. Jesus used a story with the younger son leaving and coming back because His audience, the Jewish culture, would understand what the story implied and what I am about to tell you. In the Jewish culture, the oldest son would automatically receive a double portion. If you remember, the older son did not leave, but it was the younger son that left and returned. You will also remember that when he left, he took his legal share of the estate, his legal portion, with him. He now had no further claim on the estate or anything in it. But when the younger son returned and the father reinstated him as a son and, specifically, gave him the fatted calf to celebrate his return, the older son was furious. In the older son's mind, that calf belonged to him as it was part of his portion of the estate.

So here is the point. Although the younger brother had already received his share of the estate, he was reinstated as a son and now was enjoying a second portion. This would mean that he actually received a double portion of the estate. From the older brother's perspective, this was not fair, and in anger, he tells his father so. He claims that he has been faithful to labor for him all these years and that this younger brother has done nothing but disgrace the family. Why would he then get a double portion?

So was this fair? From the perspective of the earth curse system of painful toil and sweat, we would all say it was not. We would probably side with the older son who had faithfully labored and could make a claim of injustice on the grounds of what he had done for his father.

But on what basis do we judge what is fair? Is it not the father who judges and decides to whom He wants to show His favor? The earth curse system training we would have all had would imply that if the father gave the younger son another portion of the estate, the older son would have to do with less. But this is not the case. The father is so wealthy that even the servants have more than enough. How much more for the sons.

Satan does not want you to know just how great our God is or who you really are. He has been perpetuating lies about our Father from the beginning. Insurance policies claim that when disasters strike they are an act of God. Religious organizations claim that God is pleased with a vow of poverty. People claim that God does bad things to good people. Satan would have you blind to who you are and how great your Father is less you come to your senses and return to Him with all your heart. I can assure you that when you do turn to Him, you will find the same reception that greeted this young son in the story.

"Who is the older son?" you say. Let's see if you can figure it out.

> *Meanwhile, the older son was in the field. When he came near the house, he heard music and dancing. So he called one of the servants and asked him what was going on. "Your brother has come," he replied, "and your father has killed the fattened calf because he has him back safe and sound."*
>
> *The older brother became angry and refused to go in. So his father went out and pleaded with him. But he answered his father, "Look! All these years I've been slaving for you and never disobeyed your orders. Yet you never gave me even a young goat so I could celebrate with my friends. But when this son of yours who has squandered your property with prostitutes comes home, you kill the fattened calf for him!"*
>
> *"My son," the father said, "you are always with me, and everything I have is yours. But we had to celebrate and be glad, because this brother of yours was dead and is alive again; he was lost and is found."*

The older son says that during all these years he has been slaving for his father, yet during all that time, not once did his father give him even a young goat to celebrate with his friends. Let me interpret what he is saying. "Father, you are unfair!" But notice what the father says in return.

SATAN DOES NOT WANT YOU TO KNOW JUST HOW GREAT OUR GOD IS OR WHO YOU REALLY ARE.

"You are always with me, and EVERYTHING I HAVE is yours."

Stop!!!!

Now, can you figure out who the older son is? The older son has been too busy slaving for his father with a wrong perception of self-righteousness to actually enjoy his father's goodness. Everything that father has has been his all along.

You're right, the older son represents the law of the first covenant. The first son could never enjoy the benefits of his father's house because he was too busy working for his father's approval. Although the older son had a right to the double portion, it was only the younger son that actually enjoyed it.

You are the younger son!

You have the double portion. You are the son that is received not based on what you do but based on who you are in Christ—a son or daughter of God, enjoying an inheritance you did not have to work for but freely receive from your Father.

CHAPTER 9
MORE THAN ENOUGH!

I understand that you may be skeptical of the title of this chapter, but this is where you are headed, more than enough. Not because I am showing you the latest, hottest moneymaking scheme but because as a child of God it is your legal right to enjoy the goodness and the prosperity of your Father's house. The concept of the double portion, having more than enough, may seem impossible to envision right now compared to where you see yourself at this moment in your life. But that is where you need to start your journey to freedom—in your thinking. Unless your thoughts agree with the Word of God, you will never enjoy His benefits. So lift your eyes from what you see around you and set them on what God says is yours in His Kingdom. Stop

THE CONCEPT OF THE DOUBLE PORTION, HAVING MORE THAN ENOUGH, MAY SEEM IMPOSSIBLE TO ENVISION RIGHT NOW COMPARED TO WHERE YOU SEE YOURSELF AT THIS MOMENT IN YOUR LIFE. BUT THAT IS WHERE YOU NEED TO START YOUR JOURNEY TO FREEDOM—IN YOUR THINKING.

arguing with what God is saying because you do not see it in your life. Instead, start arguing with your circumstances with the Word of God, believing that they must line up with all that God says is yours. I am just a guy like you that simply did what I am telling you to do. Believe what God says! God's Word cannot fail and it will bring a change to any circumstance. For instance, here is an email I received from a listener who was skeptical, she had heard it all, or had she?

"I am going to try to put 22 years of struggling in as few sentences as possible. Both my husband and I grew up in Christian families and attended church regularly. We were even involved in youth, Sunday school, etc. When we got married, our first year financially was good … that was over 22 years ago. Since then, the "money thing" was a constant source of pain and struggle, and my faith was always wavering because I could not understand why what the Scriptures said was supposed to happen didn't. If God's Word was eternal and imperishable and He is the same yesterday, today, and forever, then what gives? Either He was a martyr, a liar, or a lunatic!

"Fast forward to January 28th, 2013 … I told my husband, 'Either God shows up or I walk away.' … I was done with church and God. When I left the house to run a few errands, my husband finally heeded to the Holy Spirit's urging and called a dear friend of ours to talk. After he finished, she said that she had something for us to listen to—Gary Keesee. She shared her testimony on what happened to her. So, when I got home my husband told me what she had said and that he was going over the next day to pick it up.

"I don't know what happened (because I had heard enough from pastors and teachers about all the "spiritual stuff"), but I called her up, and asked if she was available that evening. In the midst of a very snowy night, I managed to get to her house. While I was driving, I told God, 'This had better be it!'

"The next day, we started listening, and the both of us were completely overwhelmed. It all started to make sense. All those verses: faith, holding fast to your confession. All the pieces of the puzzle were finally in place. We had heard about the Kingdom a few years back, <u>BUT</u> no one bothered to teach the PROCESS ... how to get to the 'THERE IT IS!' You did.

"So immediately, we put into practice what we learned ... we needed money for our mortgage payment. It was Thursday, and my husband had finished some small jobs at my parents' house... they kept asking me how much should they give my husband (they knew things were tough). I told them, 'Whatever they wanted.' It wasn't enough to pay the mortgage payment ... BUT it was still only Thursday.

"Friday, we had scheduled an appointment to meet with the friend who lent us the CDs. There was a major snowstorm, but both my husband and I wanted to sit down and talk to her about the Kingdom and how it operated.

"Before we left, she wanted to pray, and she handed us a check ... the Lord had impressed on her heart to sow into our lives. That completely floored us. Then we opened the check ... it was MORE THAN ENOUGH to pay the mortgage and other smaller bills!

"I told my husband this was all I needed! I took a picture of the check to remind me of His faithfulness. Well, the enemy didn't like what he saw and immediately (and boy, do I mean immediately!!!!) tried to steal our seed. We had decided this was the truth, and we were not going to speak anything that would destroy our future. He was relentless ... but we kept our heels buried in and our shield up.

"(Now before I go on, I need you to understand that I was a hardheaded Italian who was fed up of the 'prosperity teachings' I had heard ... and my husband knew this. The true miracle was that I fully grasped it and held onto it ... sometimes my husband looks at me and wonders what the heck happened!

"We released our faith and sowed to receive a contract for our construction company on 3/13 for an immediate contract of $150,000 to pay off overdue bills, taxes, etc. On April 5/13, we received two contracts totaling $450,000 in ONE DAY!!!!! This was only after two months since we began to apply the Kingdom principles.

"We got our children involved and they saw the 'there it is.' Now, they've made their own list and sown from their piggy banks to seed for what they want. We have verses in every room, and our five-year-old goes to them and declares, 'I believe I have received it.'

"We are so grateful that we now have more money to give and that we are one day closer to being debt free and being able to complete our assignments!

"Thank, Pastor Gary, for taking the time to reply to emails that I had sent you. We understand that your time is limited, and the fact that you took the time to do this shows how much you want to share this incredible message of God's great Kingdom."

I get emails like this every day. People like you and me are discovering the truth about who they are in Christ, learning how the Kingdom of God functions, and enjoying the benefits. So how did Drenda and I discover the principle of the double portion? I am going to tell you in this chapter and know you will find our stories encouraging.

When Drenda and I began to learn the laws and principles from the Kingdom of God, our lives were radically transformed, as I told you in the first part of this book, from living hand to mouth, dealing with panic attacks, antidepressants, and extreme hopelessness to a life of purpose and provision. We saw things happen over and over again that made us stop and say, "Did you see that? Wow!" We would constantly see the Kingdom of God operate just like the Bible said, and we would ask questions, "How or why did that happen? or "What principle did we tap into?" Although we were enjoying more than enough, we really did not see the double portion as clearly as the stories I am going to show you. We were enjoying the double portion, however, we just did not know to actually call what we were seeing the double portion until God kept increasing our understanding of it. Before I explain how God helped us understand the double portion in a greater way, I want to review our key Scripture again for a minute. (The words in brackets are my notes, not part of the actual Scripture.)

> *There remains, then, a Sabbath-rest for the people of God. For anyone who enters God's rest [faith] also rests from his own work [the earth curse system of painful toil, sweat, and survival] just as God did from his [because He was finished].*
> — Hebrews 4:9-10

By now you know that this Sabbath rest is a promise to every New Testament believer in Christ and it is not just an Old Testament thing. You also now know that the Sabbath is not possible without having more than enough, or as we saw in Exodus 16, the double portion. Please do not confuse walking in the double portion to mean that you will in every case have a huge cash surplus on hand when God asks you to move on a project.

There have been times in my life when Jesus told me to move forward on a project when I did not have any of the money in the bank. I realized later that God was never nervous about the money and knew where it would come from. But He did not allow it to manifest, lest the enemy try to steal it before it was actually needed. Let me caution you, only make a decision to move forward in a situation like that if you are sure you have heard from the Holy Spirit to do so. Again, unless Jesus tells you to move forward on a project without the funds in place, do not move forward on it. Wait until the timing of God and the provision to be available.

In general, we as believers are called to live out of the financial overflow of our lives. We are not paupers but able to be generous on every occasion just as our Father is. I only mention that because I have received so many emails where people jumped out there and missed God's timing. Listen, just because God shows you something does not mean it is time to move on it. Many times, He shows you something to give you direction and time for preparation. In my experience, timing is just as important as hearing direction in the first place.

When Jesus began His ministry in His hometown, after He had been baptized in the river Jordan by John the Baptist and after the 40 days and nights in the wilderness, He went into His local synagogue and picked up the scroll of Isaiah and turned to the sixty-first chapter and read. We find this event recorded in Luke 4:18–21.

> *The Spirit of the Lord is on me, because he has anointed me to preach good news to the poor. He has sent me to proclaim freedom for the prisoners and recovery of sight for the blind, to release the oppressed, to proclaim the year of the Lord's favor.*
>
> *Then he rolled up the scroll, gave it back to the attendant and sat down. The eyes of everyone in the synagogue were fastened on him, and he began by saying to them, "Today this scripture is fulfilled in your hearing."*

Of course, they were furious at Him for implying that He was the one it was referring to. But pay close attention to where Jesus stopped reading. Verses one to two of Isaiah 61 actually say,

> *He has sent me to bind up the brokenhearted, to proclaim freedom for the captives and release from darkness for the prisoners, to proclaim the year of the Lord's favor and the day of vengeance of our God.*

Notice Jesus stopped in the middle of a sentence. He did not read, "and the day of vengeance of our God." Why? Because He wanted to stop on the first part of that sentence, "the year of the Lord's favor." What is the year of the Lord's favor? The Year of Jubilee! Jesus was basically declaring that everything the shadow of the Sabbath Day, the Sabbath Year, and the Year of Jubilee showed us was now fulfilled and now here because He had come. The entire chapter of Isaiah 61 tells us what Jesus has done for us. In regard to the double portion, take a look at verses seven through nine.

> *Instead of their shame my people will receive a double portion, and instead of disgrace they will rejoice in their inheritance; and so they will inherit a double portion in their land, and everlasting joy will be theirs. For I, the Lord, love justice; I hate robbery and iniquity. In my faithfulness I will reward them and make an everlasting covenant with them. Their descendants will be known among the nations and their offspring among the peoples. All who see them will acknowledge that they are a people the Lord has blessed.*
>
> — Isaiah 61:7-9

I certainly understand having shame because of debilitating financial issues. So many times I found myself humiliated and embarrassed over our financial situation. I remember one time I had gathered about 20 of our friends out to a dinner in a local restaurant. I do not remember the special occasion we were celebrating, but I

> JUST BECAUSE GOD SHOWS YOU SOMETHING DOES NOT MEAN IT IS TIME TO MOVE ON IT. MANY TIMES, HE SHOWS YOU SOMETHING TO GIVE YOU DIRECTION AND TIME FOR PREPARATION.

had agreed to pay for the event. I remember being so uptight during the meal because I really did not have the money to host such an event. The money I had expected to show up from a business deal I was working on had been delayed. The only credit card I had was not canceled, but it was maxed out and I was not sure if it would work one more time or not. Sure enough, at the end of the meal the card was declined. I had to humbly ask, with great humiliation, one of my guests to pay for the event.

Oh, I have many stories like that, but I am not sure you have enough tissues nearby to embark on such an accounting. But praise God, through Jesus, all who see us will have to acknowledge that we are a people the Lord has blessed!

The double portion is yours, Jesus is your Sabbath rest, and He is your double portion! If you have read any of my previous books, you know that the Lord taught me a lot about the Kingdom through deer hunting. In fact, deer hunting was the vehicle that God used to first catch my attention with the Kingdom. I had been deer hunting for a number of years with no success. Although I was putting time and money into my efforts, I ended up with no success and no venison. To be quite honest, I never even had a shot. This particular year as I was thinking about the upcoming deer hunting season, God spoke to me and said, "Why don't you let me help you with your deer hunting this year?!" Of course, I had no idea what that meant, but He told me to take a check and write, "For my 1987 buck" on it in the memo section, along with a certain amount of money, and then mail it to a ministry where He was directing me to send it. He also told me to have Drenda and I lay our hands on that check and claim Mark 11:24 as we prayed over it.

Mark 11:24 says,

> *Therefore I tell you, whatever you ask for in prayer, believe that you have received it, and it will be yours.*

To make a long story short, I went out to a totally unfamiliar piece of property that year and had my buck in about 40 minutes. Drenda and I have followed these steps for the last 30 years, and I have always harvested my deer in 30 to 40 minutes every year since then. Through the years, I have seen God do some pretty amazing things while out hunting, and I have learned quite a few lessons about the laws of the Kingdom through hunting as well. (All of those early stories are recorded in my book *Faith Hunt*.)

I usually prefer to bow hunt in the warm fall colors then to hunt in the cold gun season here in Ohio. The limit on the number of deer you can harvest is quite generous in Ohio, and in any given year, the limit is six deer a year. I have never had to harvest that many deer to feed my family. My freezer is usually pretty full with two or three deer a year. To appreciate what I am about to tell you, you need to know that while hunting all those years I had never shot two deer from the same tree in the same morning or evening hunt. By the way, if you are not a hunter, yes, we bow hunt from a tree stand. Typically, when I killed a deer, I would leave the woods and come back out another day and take another one. But the Lord wanted to teach me something on this particular evening hunt.

It was one of those perfect fall hunting days, a bit of cloud cover and a light drizzle dampened the ground from time to time. It was a Sunday evening, I was a bit tired from conducting multiple church services that morning, and I was looking forward to being in the woods. Drenda was heading out to do some shopping for a few things, and she and I had agreed that this would be a good night to put some venison in the freezer. I was putting my camo on and gathering up my things as she went out to the car. I came outside just as she was starting the car to pull out. As she started the car, she rolled the window down and said to me, "The double portion." I did not know why she said that, although later she said that she heard the Lord say that to her at that moment and felt led to tell me that.

We had sown for three deer that year, and this was the first day out hunting for that season. I gave her a quick kiss and told her I agreed, and I headed out toward our woods. I hunt my own property, so I was very familiar with where I was headed. As I climbed up into my tree stand, I gave my grunt call a couple of blows. Within 15 minutes, a large 8-point came running in, I took a 40-yard shot, and my buck was down. That was awesome! I climbed down and walked out to the buck, but then I remembered what Drenda had said, the double portion, so I left the buck where he had fallen and walked back to my tree and climbed back up into the stand.

I thought with all the commotion that I had made getting down, walking around, and then walking back to the stand and climbing up, let alone all the scent I had probably scattered around, that in the natural there would be a slim chance of another kill in the few remaining minutes of legal shooting light. But within 15 minutes of being in the tree, a button buck walked directly under my tree, and I dropped him with a perfect shot. Wow, two shots and two deer in a row from the same tree. I had never done that before. That caught my attention and I knew it was the double portion Drenda had spoken of.

For the next five years, I had the same experience. Every time I went out bow hunting, I would now get two deer out of the same tree minutes apart. I knew this was not normal, and I began to dwell on the double portion, realizing that once again God was teaching me yet another lesson about His Kingdom.

I have always loved guns and, of course, I love to hunt. I have my own collection of guns that I use in hunting, and I was pretty happy with the guns I owned. Drenda and I have 60 acres of land with about 25 acres of woods and another 15 acres of marsh. In any given fall, the marsh can be dry or full of water, depending on how wet the summer was.

This particular year, we had quite a wet summer, so the marsh was full of water as the fall duck season came in. There were always ducks coming into the marsh any year there was water, but I had really not paid much attention to them. But this year there were large flocks coming into the marsh with the water being so high, and I could not resist. Although I never set out to hunt them in the past, I thought I would go down to the marsh and try some duck hunting. Well, the hunting was great. There were ducks everywhere, and we had a few duck dinners that year.

While hunting ducks that year, I found that many times the ducks were passing just out of shotgun range. I was using my everyday, all-around shotgun I usually used for rabbits and pheasants, but as the ducks flew just outside of shotgun range, I remembered that I had heard of a newer type of shotgun that was designed just for duck hunting. They were camouflaged and were able to shoot the new duck loads that carried a much larger load of shot, which allowed for much longer shots. I remember thinking I should check into them sometime.

Well, it just happened that I was in a local sporting goods store a month after the duck season ended when I spotted a rack of guns labeled waterfowl guns. I looked at them for bit, but with a $2,000 price tag and the fact that I would not need the gun for another 10 months when duck season reopened, I decided to wait on the purchase. But without thinking, I said out loud, "Lord, I would like that one." I did not think much about it as I left the store, but a few weeks later I was speaking at a corporate sales meeting, not a church meeting, a corporate sales meeting. At the end of my presentation, the CEO thanked me for speaking and said, "We wanted to thank you for speaking tonight with a gift." I was in shock as he brought out the exact shotgun I had looked at in the sporting goods store only a few weeks earlier. My words, "Lord, I'll take that one," and the fact that I had given guns away in the past brought that harvest.

In the first book of this series, *Your Financial Revolution: the Power of Allegiance*, I talk about the principle that caused that gun to show up. I call it the sickle principle, and it is found in Mark 4:26–29. I would suggest getting a copy of the book if you have not already read it. That gun showing up was amazing for sure, but it is not the real story I want to focus on. But it did prompt the story I want to tell you.

After that gun showed up, and I realized how I had put that harvest into motion, I thought for a moment one day about any other guns I thought I would like to own. After all, I had sown dozens of guns, so I thought I would experiment with the laws of the Kingdom. The only gun that I did not have in my collection was an over and under shotgun. They are beautiful shotguns, and usually they are not cheap either. So I said, "Lord, I would like to have one of those nice over and under shotguns!"

About a month later, I received a call from a partner of the ministry, and he said that he wanted to buy me a shotgun, an over and under. I was thrilled and he said he would be sending it by mail. Well, a few days later I received two beautiful over and under shotguns in the mail, just gorgeous! Notice that I received two shotguns. "Wow," I thought. I called the partner up and thanked him for the beautiful shotguns he had sent. In a few days he sent two more. When I called to thank him again, he said, "I was so impressed that you actually called me personally to thank me, I wanted to send you two more." I was overwhelmed with the gifts, but I was beginning to see a pattern here. Two shotguns each time? Sounds like the double portion.

About two months ago, I was teaching at a church in the morning and then I was to teach in the same city at a different church that night. After the morning service, a man walks up to me and says, "I am going to send you a beautiful Browning semiautomatic shotgun I have." Again, I was thrilled. Strangely, in the evening service at the other church, a man walks up and says, "I brought a brand-new rifle that is still in the box that I want to give you." It was a beautiful, scoped out Marlin 30/30, a gun that I have often admired but have never owned. Again, I was surprised but I was catching on—the double portion.

Again, not a few weeks after that, the same thing happened—two shotguns were given to me in the same day. Well, all I can say is I am a man blessed with great shotguns for sure. But like every story I tell, I always ask, "How did that happen?" Of course, I have already told you that I have sown many guns in the past but never said," I'll take that one, Lord," until then. Again, this is the sickle principle that you need to know. But past the sickle principle, I was tapping into the double portion in a very distinct and obvious way and I wanted to know exactly how I was doing that. I believe the Lord showed me that so many of us have missed this very important aspect of reaping from the Kingdom, and I am going to spend some time in the next chapter dealing with that topic. But before I do, I just have to share with you how that year continued to play out.

After I had received the shotguns in the mail, this story happened—and it is one of the most amazing stories that has happened in regard to seeing the double portion show up in a clear, obvious, no questions asked, this is a double portion example. This story has to do with my vehicles, specifically my pearl white Cadillac Escalade that was given to me that I mentioned a few chapters ago.

As I said earlier in the book, Drenda and I are not really into cars. We usually just drive them until they stop working or just do not look good.

And again in this story, I need to mention that Drenda and I had given several cars away before and had not really put a clear demand on our faith as to what we were believing to reap from that giving. But if you remember that story, when we drove that rented Escalade during our conference and said, "We like this; we think we should get one of these," we were not really expecting someone to just call us up and say they wanted to buy us one. But, of course, that is what happened. And, of course, we had not told anyone that we wanted one. So as I told you earlier, the pearl white, short version Escalade showed up and it was and is just awesome. I love it.

But there is an even more amazing side note to that story that occurred just this past summer. We had driven this Escalade for about a year and a half by the time last summer arrived, and one day I noticed

I PURSUE THE KING AND HIS KINGDOM, BUT IN THE KINGDOM I FIND MORE THAN ENOUGH, THE DOUBLE PORTION!

that the check engine light came on. "No big deal," I thought, but I wanted to have it checked out, so I had a dealer take a look at it. They said it was really not an issue. The sensor was picking up a tiny bit of oil in the exhaust, but it would not cause a problem. The engine would last as long as I wanted to drive it. I asked them why it would be picking up oil. My escalade had a custom aftermarket exhaust system put on it, and they thought that that could be a reason why it was showing up. Again, they said the engine itself was fine and I should expect the engine to last a long time.

One day, in a casual conversation with the man that had given me the vehicle, I mentioned the sensor light issue I was having. He said, "Yes, I have seen that happen with some other GMC vehicles." "In fact," he said, "it is quite common in the older ones." He went on to say that it would not affect the car in any way and that I should be able to drive the vehicle for the next 10 years or longer with no problem.

He knew that Drenda and I have a house in Florida that I had just purchased. I sat there stunned as he then said, "I will tell you what. You drive this one down to Florida and use it down there, and I will buy you another one to drive up here in Ohio." Yes, I now have two pearl white, short version Escalades that are perfect in every way, besides the sensor light that comes on once in a while in the first one. They are both perfect in every way! Again, it was one of those, "Did you see that?" moments. Drenda and I have to pinch ourselves as we drive those beautiful vehicles. We did not pay for either one of those vehicles. But in this case, we knew it was the double portion.

I am not telling you these stories to brag in any way, but friend, I am blessed! I am enjoying the double portion, which is as you now know, having more than enough. I have a gun safe full of guns, which are more than enough. I have two identical Escalades that I did not pay for. I think you would agree that is more than enough! And it is not that I am encouraging you to seek material things, I am not. I hold things loosely, and I do not worship stuff or pursue it. I pursue the King and His Kingdom, but in the Kingdom I find more than enough, the double portion!

Wait, I am not done testifying of the Lord's goodness and the double portion just yet.

My wife had wanted a beach home for the last 20 years. No, let me rephrase that. She has wanted one forever! She just loves the ocean! Anyway, she has been watching ocean property for years. In the past when there was a great deal on a home she liked, our money would be tied up in ministry projects and we would wait. Well, this year I was praying in the basement as I was riding my stationary bike. All of a sudden, the Lord impressed on me in a very strong way, "Tell

Drenda to go to Florida, to that town she has desired to have a home in, and tell her to buy her ocean home this week." Wow, this week? There was a strong urgency in my spirit when I heard that. So I told Drenda what the Lord had said to me, and we contacted a friend of ours who lived in that city to see if she would want to drive Drenda around for a few days to look at houses. She said she would love to.

So Drenda went online and made a list of about 25 homes she wanted to take a look at. Once there, Drenda narrowed her list of 25 houses down to 5 that were a possibility and one that she said she loved. At this point, I flew down and joined her and she showed me the 5 houses and the one she loved. We narrowed the 5 to 2—the one she loved and another house that was very nice but not as nice as the one she loved. I will have to admit when I saw the house that she loved, I knew it was Drenda, and we ended up putting an offer on it. The owner accepted our offer and we were in contract to close on our new home.

A few weeks after, when we were home in Ohio just resting, Drenda gasped and said, "That's my house!" "I know," I said, "This is your house. God told me that I was to buy you your ocean home the week I sent you to the ocean."

"No," she said, "You do not understand; that is my house." She went on to explain that she had been looking for homes for a number of years in that area, and one day she saw a picture of the house we were buying in a real estate ad. When she saw it, she loved it. She loved everything about it, the Spanish Mediterranean architecture, the floor plan, the location, everything. She remembered putting her finger on that picture and saying, "Lord, I want that house!" But she knew that house was too expensive and we had already committed our cash to other projects, so she kept looking at houses that were in our price range at the time. But no other house clicked, and we never got to the point of actually putting a contract on one. We just did not have peace yet about a house.

You should also know that we had sown seed for an ocean beach house in this town over two years earlier. Our confession during this time was that we have a beach house in this town, we already have it, and we received it the day that we sowed for it. I can remember the exact spot and moment that we held hands and came into agreement on behalf of Drenda's ocean beach house. But now as we were in contract, Drenda suddenly remembered the picture she had seen two years earlier and realized that this was the same house, her house!

After investigating the history of the house, we found out that the owner had indeed tried to sell the house a few years earlier, but it did not sell and he took it off the market. That was when Drenda had seen the picture of the house in its real estate listing. But the owner had decided to list it again, and this explains why I had a sudden urgency to send Drenda to the ocean with the instructions, "You are to buy a house this week." She will tell you that is not how I usually spend money. Timing is everything. This time, my money was not involved with other projects and was available for the house. I am sure that there were many people looking at that house and that was the reason for the urgency. Amazingly, the price had not gone up from the price listed two years earlier when she first saw it. I believe God was holding it for her!

But here is the double portion part of the story. While our house was in contract waiting to close, we received a call from Drenda's mother. They had owned a home in Canada for the last 32 years. We had been there a number of times over the years and loved the home and the location. The home is on an island right on the water. In fact, the ocean is about 30 feet from the back deck. Drenda's parents were getting older and decided that they did not want the upkeep and expense of a home so far away. They came to us and asked us if we had any interest in buying it and I said no. It was a 31-hour drive from Ohio, and although I loved the place, I just did not see it being something that I could get to that often due to the travel time. So they listed the house with a real estate agent, but after having it on the market for two years, no buyer showed serious interest.

So now while we were waiting to close on our ocean beach house, they called and explained that they have tried to sell the home without success and would be willing to cut the price in half if we wanted to buy it and keep it in the family. As I thought about it, my children had grown up going there and it is a beautiful place. So Drenda and I prayed about it and said we would take it. We had just enough cash on hand to make the purchase. Besides that, we had purchased a plane for my company the previous year, which allowed us to get there in 5 hours instead of the 31 hours it required by car. That made going there a lot more feasible.

DO NOT THINK THE DOUBLE PORTION IS LIMITED TO HAVING TWO OF SOMETHING. IN ACTUALITY, THE DOUBLE PORTION IS SIMPLY HAVING MORE THAN ENOUGH.

After we closed on both houses, I was sitting in my office one day when all of a sudden it hit me, "Wait a minute, this is the double portion!" My wife had been dreaming of an ocean home for years. Now, in the space of two months, she got a home that is in the southern part of the United States, which is warm in the winter but too hot to really use much in the summer. But the home in Canada is the perfect temperature in the summer but too cold in the winter. We realized that she now has an ocean house for both seasons. Incredible. We definitely said, "Did you see that?" when those two closings took place. I think you would agree this looks and smells like the double portion! Amazing!

I have used several examples of how God brought two of something to Drenda and me, which I believe God used to let us clearly see the double portion in operation. But I want to make sure that you do not think the double portion is limited to having two of something. In actuality, the double portion is simply having more than enough. God was using these very distinct examples of two of something to catch my attention about the double portion. So no matter what it is, having it abundantly supplied is the double portion. I hope you are catching the reality of the double portion and the Sabbath rest. Life is so amazing in the Kingdom! As I write this chapter, I am sitting in our home in Canada, looking out the window at the ocean. There are sea gulls and ducks playing along the shore only 25 yards from the house. There is peace, no striving, it is paid for, and a blessing. I am on assignment, sharing the good news of my Father's Kingdom, a son in His house, a citizen of His great Kingdom, and I am enjoying the double portion!

Drenda and I could write so many stories of how the Kingdom of God and the laws that govern it have impacted our lives, as well as the thousands of people that email us with their stories. As I shared, you can read all these things in the Bible, but it is so exciting to see the Bible play out before your eyes.

Just a side note I would like to add here. It is really quite a gamble on my part to tell people how God has blessed Drenda and me and the journey we have walked out. People many times take it wrong. They sometimes may think we are prideful or bragging. Or they think that we have taken their tithe money or their offerings and spent it on ourselves. Please understand that Drenda and I take no money from our TV broadcast, and we take no money from the sale of our resources. Yes, we do get a salary, of course, from the church we pastor. But we own businesses and always have, and God blesses them. I just wanted to make sure you know our hearts in sharing our personal stories. I felt that I needed to tell you what we have actually seen happen, and what God has taught us about those events. The results I am sharing with you are not Gary and Drenda Keesee's results; we are not that good! No, what we have seen and what we are enjoying is the result of our Father and His Kingdom in our lives. We share these stories because we just want you to get it! Hey, we came from nothing, and the only reason I am writing this book is for you! I want you to know how it works so that you can understand and receive all God has for you as well.

Understand that I hate poverty with a passion. Those nine years of living in constant stress and fear were a living hell on earth, literally! I hope you will remember that the Sabbath rest is yours as well as mine! In the next chapter, I am going to help you understand how to tap into the Sabbath rest.

Just a side note to this chapter. As I just finished writing the above sentence, my secretary came into my office and said a box had arrived for me. I was surprised to open it and find two very nice shotguns. Wow, that was encouraging! It was just as if God was putting the "Amen" on what I had just said.

After this book went to print and I had received the first truckload of books, I was excited to teach these principles for the first time at our Atlanta Revolution conference. I was also excited to have my new book with me to get to the people. As I was getting ready to head down to the ballroom to speak, my secretary called me and said there was a phone call for me from the gentleman that had given me the first set of guns, and he said he needed to talk to me right away. So I gave him a quick call. He was so excited as he explained that he had just been to the UPS office and had mailed me two more guns! Besides that, he had also sent Drenda a gun, and because he knew she did not hunt, he sent her $1,500 in one hundred dollar bills. I was shocked. I felt it was God again confirming what I was doing and, in a way, telling me to keep going. People need to know this stuff—God wants you to know this! Anyway, when I got home, I was excited to open the box. Drenda and I received the most beautiful matching Browning over-and-under shotguns I had ever seen. They were both brand new. I also had a Browning gold semiautomatic 20 gauge and then, of course, Drenda had her $1,500. The double portion!

You may be wondering why so many guns. Well, I have to admit I now have a lot of very nice shotguns, not cheap ones either, and I asked the same question. God let me know that He had sent so many very expensive and beautiful shotguns to let me see just how vast His resources were, that His provision is beyond what I expected and so far beyond survival. I get it! I see it!

CHAPTER 10
THE MYSTERY OF THE DOUBLE PORTION

I have now covered what the Sabbath rest is and how it is possible through the double portion. The question that should be on your mind is, "How do I tap into the double portion?" Well, I am glad you asked! To find the answer to that question, let's go back to the story where Jesus fed the 5,000 men with five loaves and two fish.

> By this time it was late in the day, so his disciples came to him. "This is a remote place," they said, "and it's already very late. Send the people away so they can go to the surrounding countryside and villages and buy themselves something to eat."
>
> But he answered, "You give them something to eat." They said to him, "That would take eight months of a man's wages! Are we to go and spend that much on bread and give it to them to eat?"
>
> "How many loaves do you have?" he asked. "Go and see."
>
> When they found out, they said, "Five—and two fish."
>
> Then Jesus directed them to have all the people sit down in groups on the green grass. So they sat down in groups of hundreds and fifties. Taking the five loaves and the two fish and looking

up to heaven, he gave thanks and broke the loaves. Then he gave
them to his disciples to set before the people. He also divided the
two fish among them all. They all ate and were satisfied, and the
disciples picked up twelve basketfuls of broken pieces of bread and
fish. The number of the men who had eaten was five thousand.
— Mark 6:35-44

We talked earlier about this story, but there are some really big clues here about the double portion. In the story, Jesus supernaturally

THERE IS A BETTER WAY TO LIVE THAN JUST AIMING AT BEING SATISFIED. YOU CAN'T BUILD MUCH WITH A SATISFIED MIND-SET. VISION IS STILL LIMITED AT THE SATISFIED LEVEL OF FOCUSING ONLY ON TODAY.

multiplied the bread and fish, and the people all ate until they were satisfied. I am assuming there were around 20,000 people, including women and children; and that many people being fed from five loaves and two fish until everyone was full is an absolute God thing for sure. And for that, we can celebrate the Kingdom and how it operated. But just having the people fed is not the entire picture of what happened, and if you stop there, you will miss the double portion. Let's dig a bit further.

They all ate and were satisfied, and the disciples <u>picked up</u>
<u>twelve basketfuls of broken pieces of bread and fish.</u> The number
of the men who had eaten was five thousand.

So what is the text telling us? That after everyone was satisfied, 12 baskets full of bread and fish pieces were picked up. The definition of the double portion is having more than enough. Enough is being satisfied, but 12 baskets left over after the people were satisfied is the double portion, more than enough. Please let that difference settle into your consciousness for a bit. I want you to get a clear picture of satisfied verse the double portion in your mind. I do not have time here to go into much depth on how Jesus brought the power of the Kingdom into that situation to accomplish the first part of this story—5,000 people being satisfied. But you can find the full explanation in the first book of this series, called *Your Financial Revolution: The Power of Allegiance.*

Instead, I want to focus on the double portion, the overflow, and how it happened in this story. Yes, it is an amazing story—20,000 people all satisfied, wow! But there is more in the Kingdom than just being satisfied, although you certainly need to be satisfied before you can go on to the overflow. Being satisfied is great, but what about tomorrow? What I am trying to say is that if your goal is only to be satisfied, what happens when you get hungry again? Many Christians are in a state of being satisfied but miss the double portion. It is the double portion that brings the Sabbath rest of God. Being satisfied is only a temporary fix. It does not solve the provision problem. Knowing that you will become hungry again even while you are currently not hungry still opens the door to fear, causing you to run and labor with a survival mind-set. No, there is a better way to live than just aiming at being satisfied. You can't build much with a satisfied mind-set. Vision is still limited at the satisfied level of focusing only on today. Just having satisfied as a goal is still a goal of survival in the earth curse painful toil and sweat system.

Satisfied eats for today; the double portion builds a tomorrow!

Let me give you an example of how the culture and most of the church thinks. Ask anyone how they are doing financially and you will get many answers, probably not many good. But if you get a good one, someone that says, "We are going great," ask them, "So how long have you had your house paid for?" They would probably stare at you and say, "Well, my house is not paid for. I just meant we are paying all our bills and have some money in the bank." "Great!" you say, "You guys are really doing well. Tell me, do you have over $10,000 in the bank?" Of course, no one would ask this, I suppose, but if you did and they would answer, they would say, "No, but we have $800." Seriously, these people think they are doing great financially because they have a nice car, a nice house, and a few bucks in the bank. They are living the satisfied lifestyle. But there is more! How about having your house paid for with $100,000 in the bank, or $500,000 in the bank? That would be a more than enough picture of life for most people. Satisfied is great and necessary, but having 12 baskets of bread and fish in the food pantry is more than enough, and there is peace!

I sat down with a client one day and was discussing his finances with him. As I was going through his debts, I noticed that he had about $40,000 in credit card debt. And as I was going through his assets, I noticed that he had about $40,000 in cash in his checking account. "Joe," I said, "this is a no brainer. You have the cash to pay off your three credit cards completely. Your interest rate on the credit card debt is 18%, and your checking account interest rate is 1%. Pay off the credit cards with the cash! But do you know what? Joe said he did not want to do that. I sat there puzzled, and asked him why. He said that having the cash in his checking account made him feel safe and financially wealthier. I just looked at him. "What do you mean it makes you feel wealthy? This is an illusion. Although you do have the $40,000 in your checking account, you really do not have

$40,000 because you owe your credit card companies $40,000. Your perception is false, and you are paying a lot of money to believe a deception."

We talked for about an hour, and he never could understand why he should consider at least putting the large majority of the contents of his checking account against the debt, which he reminded me that he had worked hard for. I gave up after another hour and went home. He was deceived; he had no security in trying to keep that money in his checking account. Oh, I know it felt good when that statement came in the mail and it showed that $40,000 in the bank. But to get a true picture of where he was, he needed to open the credit card bills as well.

Satisfied is great, and it can lure you into a false sense of security. You need to look down the road a bit and know that what you just consumed will not be able to provide for what you need in a few hours. You will be hungry again. If you are only looking for the quick fix, the quick satisfaction of provision, you are going to miss the only thing that actually can change your life—the double portion.

When we all grew up in the earth curse financial system of painful toil and sweat, we dreamed of one thing, stopping! I mentioned this in a previous chapter. We did not dream of more work or another opportunity because, quite frankly, we were already overwhelmed with life and just holding out until the next vacation. You see, slaves do not dream of more work. Slaves dream of one thing—Friday night, not Monday morning. Why? Because slaves dream of only one thing—stopping. Listen, the overwhelmed and "can't wait to stop" mind-set is never going to take you anywhere. Even if an angel came into your bedroom and told you an idea from God, your mind-set would still hold you back. Write this down.

YOU MUST SEE PAST BEING SATISFIED TO CAPTURE THE DOUBLE PORTION!

This statement is the key to the double portion. I know it does not make a lot of sense right now, but it will. To show you what I mean, I want to take one more look at the story of feeding the 5,000 people from the book of John, instead of the book of Mark. In John's perspective of the story, we find the same story but with a few details that we do not find in Mark's version.

> *Jesus then took the loaves, gave thanks, and distributed to those who were seated as much as they wanted. He did the same with the fish. When they had all had enough to eat, he said to his disciples, "Gather the pieces that are left over. Let nothing be wasted."*
>
> — John 6:11-12

In this version of the story, we see that it was Jesus that told them to go and gather the pieces, or fragments, and let nothing be wasted. I want you to get this. He had to tell them to do that because they did not see the opportunity. Put yourself in their shoes. You are full and satisfied, and all you want to do is to lie down and take a nap. Because of your earth curse training and your slavery mentality, when you are satisfied, it is time to stop. You see, the slave mentality works only when it has to, and when it doesn't have to, when it is satisfied, it stops. Jesus had to tell them to gather what was right in front of their eyes. The fragments were all around them on the ground, yet they made no effort to pick them up. But then again, in their minds, what were fragments worth anyway but to be left for the birds?

Jesus was trying to teach them something, something very important. Jesus makes a comment after He tells them to gather the pieces, to let nothing be wasted! But what does that mean? Everyone is full, everyone is satisfied, and no one wants more bread and fish, well at least right now. But here is the problem—there is no Sabbath rest without gathering more than you need. When the Israelites gathered the manna on the sixth day, they were instructed to gather more than they needed. Them gathering more than they needed on that day became their provision on the seventh day, the day of rest. Jesus was teaching His disciples to look past being satisfied and to see the full provision of the Kingdom. Again, you cannot build with satisfied, but you can build with the double portion. Satisfied has consumed today's bread but 12 baskets left over gives you options for tomorrow.

Here is the key principle that I what you to see.

Although the disciples did not see the fragments until Jesus pointed them out, God **had already given them the Sabbath rest**, the double portion. They just did not see it. The Kingdom had already provided the food, multiplied the bread and fish, and fed all those people—but the Kingdom always supplies the double portion. God is never going to just supply satisfied; **He will always supply more than enough**. The issue is you may not be seeing it!

> *Give, and it will be given to you. A good measure, pressed down, shaken together and running over, will be poured into your lap. For with the measure you use, it will be measured to you.*
> — Luke 6:38

Give and it will be given to you, good measure, pressed down, shaken together. But this is not where this verse stops. Your measure pressed down and shaken together is your provision for that day.

But the verse goes on to say, "and running over!" The running over is the double portion. God always supplies the double portion, never just enough!!!! But if you were not aware of that, and the grain is running over, you might just let it fall to the ground as you were totally focused on the satisfied portion in front of you and not prepared to capture the overflow. In so doing, you would fail to capture and enjoy the double portion. But if you realized how the Kingdom operates, knowing about and anticipating the full provision, you would be prepared to act and capture all that God provides.

Let me give you another example.

> *Simon answered, "Master, we've worked hard all night and haven't caught anything. But because you say so, I will let down the nets." When they had done so, they caught such a large number of fish that their nets began to break. So they signaled their partners in the other boat to come and help them, and they came and filled both boats so full that they began to sink. When Simon Peter saw this, he fell at Jesus' knees and said, "Go away from me, Lord; I am a sinful man!" For he and all his companions were astonished at the catch of fish they had taken, and so were James and John, the sons of Zebedee, Simon's partners.*
>
> — Luke 5:5-10

This is a portion of the story we read earlier. Peter had two boats that almost sank with fish because of the Kingdom. This was contrary to his understanding of fishing and it astonished him. But what would happen the next time Jesus said, "Hey, Peter, go out there in the deep water, and you will be able to catch as many fish as you want"? Do you think he would take two boats? I doubt it. He would gather as many boats as he could borrow from his friends. Why? Because he would have a different expectation and knowledge of how the Kingdom operates.

The point of this whole discussion is to make sure you understand that you are not seeing all of the provision that God is sending. Of course, most of the time that provision will not be in the form of raw dollar bills. But it will be in the form of ideas, divine appointments, and direction by the Holy Spirit. If we are not prepared with a proper understanding of the double portion, we will walk right by them because of our earth curse survival training.

In the story of the bread multiplying, Jesus is trying to teach His disciples how the Kingdom operates, what to expect, and what to anticipate. Because their slavery mind-set did not see the potential of all the bread lying around, He had to coach them to look: "What do you see? Look! You are not seeing all of what God has prepared for you."

I want to remind you of Exodus 16 for a moment as there is one more thing I want to point out.

> *Each morning everyone gathered as much as he needed, and when the sun grew hot, it melted away. On the sixth day, they gathered twice as much—two omers for each person—and the leaders of the community came and reported this to Moses. He said to them, "This is what the Lord commanded: 'Tomorrow is to be a day of rest, a holy Sabbath to the Lord. So bake what you want to bake and boil what you want to boil. Save whatever is left and keep it until morning.'"*
>
> *So they saved it until morning, as Moses commanded, and it did not stink or get maggots in it. "Eat it today," Moses said, "because today is a Sabbath to the Lord. You will not find any of*

> *it on the ground today. Six days you are to gather it, but on the seventh day, the Sabbath, there will not be any."*
>
> *Nevertheless, some of the people went out on the seventh day to gather it, but they found none. Then the Lord said to Moses, "How long will you refuse to keep my commands and my instructions? Bear in mind that the Lord has given you the Sabbath; that is why on the sixth day he gives you bread for two days. Everyone is to stay where he is on the seventh day; no one is to go out." So the people rested on the seventh day.*
>
> — Exodus 16:21-30 (the manna)

As we have been saying, the double portion is what made the Sabbath rest possible. But amazingly, although God had already supplied the double portion on the sixth day, many of them went out looking for it and found none on the Sabbath. It's not that God was not faithful to supply it. They just did not see it because they did not have a proper understanding of the double portion already given on the sixth day. They had only gathered enough for one day, as usual. Now, being hungry on the seventh day, they did not find any at all. Maybe from their perspective God had failed them. But God had not failed; they had simply not been aware of the double portion principle. If they would have known, they would have planned differently.

How many people today are wandering around trying to find what they need, not realizing that God has already sent it? I think it is really interesting in this passage that God is actually mad at them for not gathering enough!!!! I wonder how that would preach in our churches.

> *Now he who supplies seed to the sower and bread for food will also supply and increase your store of seed and will enlarge*

the harvest of your righteousness. You will be made rich in every way so that you can be generous on every occasion.

— 2 Corinthians 9:10-11

Paul is pretty plain here as he explains the Kingdom of God's effect as being made rich in every way so that you can be generous on every occasion. My friend, that requires the double portion. You can't be generous on every occasion without more than enough.

In an earlier chapter, I shared with you how my business went from running at a 3 to 4 million dollar a year production level with one of our vendors to running over 11 million a year with the same vendor. All of this increase happened within just one year. I also told you how that happened, that God gave me a dream in the night and told me how to do it. But now I need to tell you what He told me because now it will make sense to you. In my dream, He simply gave me three words. That's right, just three words. Those three words changed my income by hundreds of thousands of dollars that year without me doing any more marketing or advertising than I was already doing. I changed nothing about my company's operation except me. Those three words gave me instruction to change how I personally was doing something, and that change more than quadrupled our business and my income. "What are the three words?" you ask. Simply this—Seize the Moment!

Yes, seize the moment. "That's it? Those three words did all of that?" Yep, they did. Once you understand that God ALWAYS sends the double portion with His provision, you will understand what He was telling me.

My company, like all sales companies, makes its profit by helping people. The better a company is at helping people, the more money they will make. Although this is true, it is also true that a lot of sales companies fail at meeting the needs of their clients either through poor follow-up and customer service or a lack of pursuing and securing new clients for the firm.

In our case, we were extremely busy, and although that was not a bad thing, we sometimes did not provide the quickest response time I would have liked to see for our clients. For me personally, I work with our investment clients and I love it. But because of my schedule, when a potential investment client calls in and is handed to me to personally reach out to, I sometimes do not get that callback done in the first 24 hours. My intentions are good, but I just do not get it done.

THE LORD WAS TELLING ME THAT THE OVERFLOW, THE SABBATH REST, WAS ALREADY THERE, HE HAD ALREADY PROVIDED IT. I WAS JUST NOT SEEING IT!

As you know, when people are asking questions, it is the company that is providing the answers that will get their business. Sometimes being late in calling back a potential client to discuss their personal investment needs can be too late. They could have called someone else who was more available to answer their questions. There are many things that can go wrong, but the solution would be to be there with the answers when people want to know.

So when the Lord gave me those three words, I knew what it meant. I had to look at things differently if I was really going to be up on that stage, in the top 10 and receive that $100,000 bonus. I had to seize the moment! So I made a change in how I did things. I made a rule that if anyone called in for investment advice, I would call them back within a couple of minutes, if possible, and I would visit with them immediately. My clients are all over the country and this commitment was the one that was going to be hard to keep. But I was committed to it. I called my company manager and told him what God had said and told him to tell all my representatives to have the same attitude of seizing every opportunity when they showed up. When the year was over, we did over the 11 million required to be in the top 10 for that vendor. But on top of that, we had also secured additional business in the millions for our other vendors.

Here is the big reveal moment. We did nothing different but simply reacted quickly when we had a client that wanted to talk to us. You see, the Lord was telling me that the overflow, the Sabbath rest, was already there, He had already provided it. I was just not seeing it!

So there is not a double portion Kingdom law of how to enact the double portion. The double portion is always there. God always provides at a double portion level.

GOD NEVER SENDS PROVISION ONLY FOR TODAY. HE ALWAYS SENDS THE DOUBLE PORTION <u>WITH IT!</u>

Again, our problem is that we just do not see the double portion.

<u>But the bigger problem is that we did not even know to look for it!!!!</u>

I love what Jesus said, "Let nothing be wasted!" God sent it all, and He wants you to have it. He was upset that people were out looking for manna on the seventh day when He had already sent it. He reminded Moses that He had sent it on the sixth day so they could capture it and enjoy the Sabbath rest. Basically, He was telling them, "The Sabbath is not for me, it is for you. That is why I sent you the double portion." You can almost hear Jesus saying the same thing. "Hey guys, pick up those fragments, and get it all. God sent it for you to pick up so that you may enjoy the double portion and find rest."

In the story of Jesus feeding the 5,000 with the five loaves and two fish, the disciples did not see the fragments. They were not even looking for them. But Jesus told them what to pick up and the harvest was not missed. Today the Holy Spirit has to help us see past satisfied and capture the double portion. He will point things out to us that we are not seeing if we will ask him. The key I hope you have learned so far is that the double portion is already given to you; you just need to capture it.

Because the double portion is the ONLY escape from the earth curse system of painful toil and sweat, Satan hates it. Oh, he may try to convince Christians that if they are just paying their bills, working two jobs to keep up, they are doing all right. But a Christian that has money to support the Kingdom of God and lives free from financial fear and worry—now that is someone he wants to stop. Satan's intent is to keep you broke all the days of your life and enslaved to a meager survival lifestyle where you have no influence. Money is influence! Satan would love to stop you from God's blessing for sure. That is why what I am about to tell you is so important for you to understand.

The double portion is hidden!

Okay, it is time to give the disciples a break. There was a reason why they did not see the overflow. Well, of course, as we have been saying, they weren't looking, but there really was another factor. You normally do not pick up the scraps! I mean, in their minds, the bread and fish pieces lying around were just scraps.

Why was the coin that Peter needed to pay his taxes hidden in a fish's mouth? Who would ever think to look there? Who would have thought that two boats of professional fishermen who had fished all night and caught nothing would catch the biggest catch of their lives at the word of a rabbi? Who would have thought that the woman in 2 Kings 4 who had no money, nothing in her house but a tiny bit of oil, and was about to declare bankruptcy would somehow have so much oil that it paid off all her debt and allowed her to live debt free? No one would have. Who would have thought that Gary Keesee, who graduated one person away from the bottom of his class, would be a millionaire today and speaking to thousands of people around the world every day? No one! In all these stories, God used the unexpected to change the situation around.

SATAN'S INTENT IS TO KEEP YOU BROKE ALL THE DAYS OF YOUR LIFE AND ENSLAVED TO A MEAGER SURVIVAL LIFESTYLE WHERE YOU HAVE NO INFLUENCE.

If the overflow, the double portion was obvious, just sitting out in the open, Satan would have seen it and would have tried to intercept it and steal it. That is why God does not reveal His treasures openly. They are hidden. Satan hates for you to be satisfied and enjoying provision, but he really hates it if you step over into the overflow and the Sabbath rest.

Let me show you something you need to understand in regard to how God works in the earth realm.

> *No, we speak of God's secret wisdom, a wisdom that has been hidden and that God destined for our glory before time began. None of the rulers of this age understood it, for if they had, they would not have crucified the Lord of glory.*
>
> — 1 Corinthians 2:7-8

This passage clearly shows us that if Satan would have known the plan of God, he would have changed tactics! This is why God has to work undercover. Satan would react to anything obvious. Your abundant provision cannot be made obvious either until the moment you will capture or harvest it for the same reason. I have a saying that I have been saying for years. God's treasures are hidden, not from you but for you.

Hidden *from* you *for* you!

Many people tell me that they wish God would not wait until the midnight hour to bring His answers. But my friend, God is not nervous. He knows when the bill is due, and it is to your benefit that God does not show His hand too early lest Satan intercept it.

> *I will give you the treasures of darkness, riches stored in secret places, so that you may know that I am the Lord, the God of Israel, who summons you by name.*
>
> — Isaiah 45:3

Riches stored in secret places? Hey, this is better than the greatest Hollywood movie script. Let me give you an example of how God helped me capture the double portion in my business life. Years ago, I was sitting down looking at my profit and loss statement for the year for my financial services company. Although I was satisfied—I was out of debt and had some money in the bank—I knew there was more. I saw so many projects I wanted to fund in the Kingdom, so much to do, and it all cost money.

As I prayed about it, the Lord began to deal with me about the term *fragments*. At first, I did not understand what He was saying, but the longer I prayed about it and listened, I got it. Fragments like in the story we just read were overlooked. Their value was looked upon as worthless—either due to the energy it would take to capture them being perceived as not worth it or their value was based on an outdated value system. Or possibly, a faulty and limited perception of their potential use limited their understanding of their possible increase in value from what their current perception was.

You have heard people say this many times I am sure, "This is just the way we have always done it." Well, I can tell you that the double portion will probably not come that way.

As I looked over the data, God opened my eyes to many fragments I was leaving on the table that I should be picking up. One of the priorities we do with every client is to do a complete data profile on them to see what assets they may have as well as their debt. We then do an analysis to look for any money we could reposition toward debt elimination. Of course, we list their current mortgage status and the interest rate, including the terms of the loan on the data sheet. At that time, we had also been advising our clients to obtain a line of credit against their home equity to pay off high interest rate credit card debt, thus dropping their net interest rate from a typical 21% rate to a 6% rate at the time. The savings just from this maneuver saved the average family $500 to $600 a month in cash flow. When this situation presented itself, we would send our clients back to their own banks to secure the consolidation loan.

As I was studying my data, the Holy Spirit pointed this mortgage issue out to me. "Why don't you handle that mortgage work?" As I thought about it, that made sense. We already had the confidence of the client; we already had their data; and finally, we were the ones that were suggesting they refinance their debt in the first place.

To handle this side of the business would require me to learn a whole new business, pass licensing and training classes, and much more. I just did not have time to do all that. But as I continued to pray about it, the Lord impressed on me to hire someone else to set up and run my mortgage company, which is what I did. Handling the mortgage work ourselves in that first year alone brought in an additional $160,000 in net income. This was money I would have never have had if I had not allowed the Holy Spirit to point out a fragment I was staring at but never saw.

I went on to capture many more items that were fragments that the Holy Spirit showed me. One fragment that I was overlooking—because of my preconceived ideas that I had learned or heard from other people saying that this area was not worth getting into—became a huge success for us. When I finally sat down and looked at it, I realized that all the information I had heard about this product area was wrong and it was, in fact, an excellent fit for our company. That fragment has actually produced more income than my core business model has, bringing in millions of dollars. It was literally a multimillion dollar fragment!

So let me make it really clear for you. The double portion is captured through revelation! Revelation is simply something that the Holy Spirit is showing you that you would not have known on your own. So the Holy Spirit reveals or opens your eyes to something that by yourself you did not know. This is called revelation knowledge.

Revelation is the key to the double portion!

People then ask me, "How do I hear the Holy Spirit? How do I hear how to capture these hidden ideas and opportunities?" Great questions. I do not have the time in this book to go in-depth regarding hearing the voice of God. So I am going to direct you to another book I have written entitled, *The Baptism of the Holy Spirit*. You can buy it through Amazon or our website. In that book, you will find more information regarding how the Holy Spirit works to reveal God's hidden plans to us, so we can prosper right here in the earth realm, right under Satan's nose; and there is nothing he can do about it. But to get you headed in the right direction, let's take a look at **1 Corinthians 14:2.**

> *For anyone who speaks in a tongue does not speak to men but to God. Indeed, no one understands him; he utters mysteries with his spirit.*

Verse 4 says,

> *He who speaks in a tongue edifies himself.*

The word edify means to bring instruction or understanding. I need that and so do you. When the Bible is speaking here of speaking in tongues or, as Paul describes it, praying in the Spirit, I want to encourage you—no matter what you have heard about this function of the Holy Spirit, whether someone has told you that it has passed away with the apostles or that it is of the devil—read your Bible! Praying in the Spirit is simply the Holy Spirit praying through you in the earth realm to bring His will to pass without the devil knowing what is going on. Praying in the Spirit is a major key in hearing revelation from heaven, and I encourage you to study what I have said. And if you have questions, get my book and I know it will help you gain more insight into this amazing function of the Holy Spirit in our lives.

I want to conclude this book with two Scripture verses that basically sum up this chapter.

> *Now to him who is able to do immeasurably more than all we ask or imagine, according to his power that is at work within us, to him be glory in the church and in Christ Jesus throughout all generations, for ever and ever! Amen.*
> — Ephesians 3:20-21

You can never ask for something that you have not thought of. I currently own two airplanes, a smaller plane that I fly for fun and my business plane that I fly anywhere in the country I go. When I was considering buying a plane for business, I was shocked at the price. Airplanes are not cheap! I began to back up and think, "I can do without a business plane. After all, it is so much money." But I was flying every week on commercial airlines, and one month I flew 23 times. It was exhausting. Yes, I could say that I had provision. All of my flights were paid for; there were no issues with the money to pay for them. But my airline travel had become anything but restful. Flights were canceled or late, and it was a mess. This was not the Sabbath rest that I needed.

Finally, I admitted that I was limiting God here. He is the God of the double portion. Drenda and I wavered on buying that plane for over a year, I am sorry to say. Finally, God got our attention on that plane and told us He had been trying to get that plane to us for two years! We repented and made our decision. We sowed our seed for the exact business plane that we wanted and needed; and when we did, we had it within two months. During that time, God gave me insight and favor with some business deals, and the money was there when I needed it.

Yes, God is the God of the double portion. Did it make a difference? Well, the difference in my life being able to fly my own plane compared to flying commercial would be like comparing having to ride your bike or driving a car to an appointment you had 50 miles away. Really! And God was trying to get that to me for two years while I just stared at satisfied and stayed blind to the double portion that God had already provided for me. I just needed to see it.

You might be driving a car so desperately in need of repair that you pray it starts when you get up. Stop looking at the empty bank account and making survival decisions based on that. Instead, let the God of the double portion show you the fragments, the hidden things that you need to know to be free and enjoy the peace and rest of the Sabbath rest. He will give you the plan and show you how to do it if you just ask Him. As Jesus said, "Let nothing be wasted!" The double portion has already been provided for you!

> *There remains, then, a Sabbath-rest for the people of God; for anyone who enters God's rest also rests from their works, just as God did from his.*
>
> — Hebrews 4:9-10

I trust this book has been a blessing to you and your walk with the Lord Jesus Christ. As I said in the book, this is the second in the "Your Financial Revolution" series. There will be a total of five, so keep watching for the next book on our website. Also, consider becoming a member of Team Revolution, our mentorship program. You can find more information concerning Team Revolution on our websites as well.

Gary and Drenda Keesee own and operate Forward Financial Group in New Albany, Ohio, 1-(800)-815-0818.

Gary and Drenda Keesee pastor Faith Life Church in New Albany, Ohio.

For more resources by Gary and Drenda Keesee, go to FaithLifeNow.com, GaryKeesee.com, or Drenda.com.